979849541I548

## What people have said about this book:

'In this follow-up to his first book, **Lewy Body Dementia, Survival and Me**, *Kevin Quaid writes from the heart about his experiences of living with LBD. Honest, moving and easy to read, his intention is to provide hope and encouragement to others on a similar journey.*'

**Ian McKeith, FRSB, FMedSci Professor of Old Age Psychiatry at Newcastle University. First President of, The Lewy Body Society UK**

'**I am KEVIN! not Lewy** *is a must-read. The title says it all: no disease should dictate who we are. Kevin Quaid's account about his journey with Lewy Body Disease is a ray of sunshine for all people directly or indirectly touched by neurodegenerative diseases.*'

**Lea Grinberg, MD, PhD John Douglas French Alzheimer's Foundation Endowed Professor Memory and Aging Center - Department of Neurology, UCSF, USA**

'*A searingly honest account of living as best one can with Lewy Body Dementia. Kevin's depiction of hope, resilience and self-awareness, while struggling with frightening hallucinations in the stillness of the night is a compelling read.*'

**Pat McLoughlin,**

**Chief Executive, The Alzheimer Society of Ireland**

'Kevin's story is an inspiration to others, honest, and gives people hope that if they also get an early diagnosis, they can lead a full life.'

**Joan Hughes,**
**Carer to a Mother with Lewy Body Dementia**

'I have always felt that those who live with the uncertainty of dementia are the bravest people I know, and in telling his story, **I am KEVIN! not Lewy**, Kevin embodies this spirit of resilience, as he inspires us all to seek new opportunities even (and perhaps especially) when faced with the most crushing adversities.'

**Professor Seán Kennelly**
**Consultant Physician in Geriatric Medicine and Director of Cognitive Clinical Trials Unit and Memory Service, Tallaght University Hospital**

'**I am KEVIN! not Lewy** is a fascinating and deeply moving personal account of the impact of Lewy body dementia. With a skilled mix of prose, poetry and photographs, Kevin uses his own experience of having the disease to illustrate the effects of different symptoms on daily life and relationships, and how best to overcome them. The book not only provides a uniquely individual insight into the disease, but also a very useful educational *resource of how to navigate the healthcare system and society – with valuable and practical tips for people with dementia, their families and carers, and professionals.'*

**John O'Brien**
**Professor of Old Age Psychiatry and NIHR National Specialty Lead for Dementia Department of Psychiatry, University of Cambridge**

*'Kevin's indomitable spirit shines through, as he shows resilience in the face of adversity and a desire to help others...his story is truly inspiring.'*

**Carol Rogan, PhD**
**Scientific Project Manager, Dementia Research Network Ireland**

*'A tale of courage and an inspiring lesson in how the human spirit is not defined by disease, even of the brain.'*

**Professor Ian Robertson, PhD**
**Co-Director, Global Brain Health Institute, Trinity College Dublin**

'Coursing through every page of this beautiful book is hope, love, and generosity. Kevin and his wife, Helena, give readers the gift of their honest experience of living with Lewy Body Dementia. In doing so, they undo the stigma of dementia and help to improve the lives of families dealing with this diagnosis.'

**Cindy Weinstein, PhD**
**Vice Provost, California Institute of Technology**
**Author, 'Finding the Right Words - A Story of Literature, Grief and the Brain'**

'Kevin's story is so honest, so personal, and so raw. While I read this book, I feel as though I can hear Kevin speak the words - a testament of how genuine this book is.'

**Caoimhe Tyndall**
**Neuroscientist, Trinity College Dublin**

'Taking the reader along the journey of learning, sharing and giving. Thanks Kevin (not Lewy)!'

**Miriam Galvin, PhD, MSc, MA**
**Associate Professor, Academic Unit of Neurology, Trinity College Dublin Senior Atlantic Fellow, Global Brain Health Institute**

*'This book gives a voice to the many others living with LBD, who may never be heard. It's a powerfully constructed manual on how to live with and understand LBD. Kevin's lived experience displays the type of clarity and courage required, to ensure no one else, like my own father, will ever be misdiagnosed or misunderstood again.'*

**Ken Greaney**
**Director, Co-founder, Lewy Body Ireland**

*'Kevin's latest book captures in words the unexpected discovery of an even bigger world that we all continue to reach for: to learn, love, grieve, share, grow closer and hold our unique personhood as precious in the fight of our life against Lewy Body Dementia.'*

**Jenni Lawson (Heckle)**
**Talking Dementia with Heckle & Jeckle Podcast, Spotify**

*'To really understand the disease, you have to understand the lived experience. Kevin gives a wonderfully written and accessible guide to Lewy Body Dementia and how to achieve in adversity. He explains how you can live life to the full whilst facing an undefeatable foe. This is a must-read for anyone facing the battle of their life, for their life.'*

**Andrew Wormald, PhD**
**Research Fellow, Lecturer, University of Limerick**

'Robin Williams did not know that he was living with one of the most common forms of dementia when he died. Kevin's honest, brave and informative account of living with Lewy Body Dementia is a window into a little-known illness and an important contribution to growing awareness of the range of often puzzling symptoms that can present with this form of dementia.'

**Ann Nolan,**
**PhD Assistant Professor in Global Health**
**Trinity Centre for Global Health, Trinity College Dublin**

'This is a story about hope; how agency, goals and actions provide a pathway to live well with a diagnosis of Lewy Body Dementia.'

**Brian Lawlor, MD, FRCPI, FRCPsych**
**Professor of Old Age Psychiatry at Trinity College Dublin. Deputy Executive Director at Global Brain Health Institute**

'Were you ever on a journey, maybe lost somewhere, and some kind person stopped to show you the way? This book from Kevin Quaid is just like that. From the very first pages, Kevin steps beside us and takes us along his journey, good and bad, and helps us learn about Lewy bodies – and life – along the way. It is hopeful and honest – and helpful. I can't think of a better travel companion on any life journey.'

**Wendy Weidner**
**Research and Policy Lead, Alzheimer's Disease International**

'This is a book of pain, despair, discovery, determination, bravery, hope, and finally life purpose. It is a must-read for all of us!'

**Jane Ryan**
**Finance & Operations Director at Edelman Dublin**

'**I am KEVIN! not Lewy** illuminates the way for others living with Lewy Body Dementia, their caregivers, family and friends. Kevin Quaid is a true source of inspiration in the face of this mysterious illness. Through his writing he gives voice and brings hope to many. We join you in the fight Kevin, in plain sight.'

**Andrew Harkin, PhD**
**Professor in Pharmacology, Trinity College.**
**Institute of Neuroscience, Trinity College Dublin**

*'Kevin brings a powerful mix of hope, honesty, positivity and wise advice to his account of journeying with LBD. As a psychologist, working with people with this complex condition I would definitely recommend it.'*

**Alison Killen,**
**Research associate at Newcastle University**

*I have known Kevin for the last three years and have been following his journey while living with LBD. In my capacity as the Manager of CareBright Community (Ireland's first purpose-built Dementia Village), we use Kevin's first book* **Lewy Body Dementia, Survival and Me** *as part of our induction programme for new employees. This is a powerful narrative in educating our people in the reality of living with LBD.*

*His second book,* **I am KEVIN! not Lewy,** *has given me a great insight into a person's life with LBD. This will enable us to learn and implement the culture change that is required to "Look at the person as he is, not as somebody living with dementia". The personhood remains as it is regardless of each and every struggle the person with LBD goes through.'*

**Nisha Joy**
**Director of Nursing, Care Bright Dementia Village, Bruff, Co Limerick**

*'Although Kevin has Lewy Body Dementia, he is a brave man who tells things as they are. A must read in support of people living with LBD such as Kevin and myself. Life is a struggle, but we keep on fighting. Thanks Kevin!'*

**Chris Maddocks**

**Dementia Advocate and Ambassador for Lewy Body Society UK**

*'Brain diseases affect people and whilst we do all we can to prevent and treat the biology of brain disease, we must never lose site of the fact that brain diseases can affect the core of who we are - as people.* **I am KEVIN! not Lewy** *is a creative, articulate and impassioned reminder of that. As a community we need to embrace what brain illnesses mean for people and what the goal of our work together should be - seldom a (better) memory test score, a change in a blood test or a lack of "decline" in a brain scan, but rather a personal goal set by the patient that defines our partnership and takes primacy as our therapeutic target.'*

**Craig Ritchie**

**Chair of the Psychiatry of Ageing, Director of the Centre for Dementia Prevention and Director of Brain Health, Scotland**

# I am KEVIN! not Lewy

❧

## Kevin Quaid

*[handwritten: Best Wishes]*

*[handwritten signature]*   *[handwritten: 19/6/2024]*

By Kevin Quaid

0035386-1526041

Email; kevinquaid9@gmail.com

ISBN -9798490314400

ISBN -9798490314400

Edited by Helen B. Medsger

# Table of Contents

# DEDICATION

I come from a fantastic family with a lot of wonderful uncles and aunts. So many of them have always been lovely to me but there is one who always stood out, my uncle, Billy Norris, to whom I dedicate this book.

When I was a small boy, he drove a big truck and often took me with him. One trip that will live with me forever was when he took me to England for a week when I was about ten years old (which is over 47 years ago now). As a small boy, you can imagine my excitement and feeling that this was so unbelievable.

Over the years when Uncle Billy and I spoke on the phone, his first words were, 'How's my favourite nephew?' (Which I cover in a chapter later in the book.) He loved the articles I wrote for the different papers and was very proud of me and never tired of telling me so. Anyone who knew Billy Norris will remember him for his fun and sense of humour. Billy could not be in a house ten minutes before the laughter would erupt, and it was infectious.

Just like my cousin, Theresa, who passed away before I published my first book, Billy didn't get to see this one. Sadly, he died in March 2020 and the worst part for me was that I was in Australia when he passed. Since that's something I will never be able to change, now is my chance to say goodbye to my favourite uncle, Billy Norris. I hope you are as proud of this book as you were of the first one.

On occasion, I still get a call from his wonderful wife, Joan, and our conversation always comes back to something funny that Billy said. He was a true gentleman and larger than life. I will miss him until the day I die.

Goodbye, Uncle Billy.

Your favourite nephew,

Kevin

An aged man is but a paltry thing.

A tattered coat upon a stick, unless

Soul clap its hands and sing, and
louder sing

For every tatter in its mortal dress.

W.B. Yeats, 'Sailing to Byzantium'

# FOREWORD

*I am KEVIN! not Lewy* is an intensely personal story, a journey of a 'discovery mission' as Kevin Quaid terms it. Living with a curious and disturbing panoply of symptoms, Kevin was determined to make sense of his experiences and find explanations, documenting each twist and turn of the complexity of his reality until he finally received a diagnosis that could explain the chaos. This is the same diagnosis, Lewy Body Dementia that led to the tragic suicide of Robin Williams[1] in 2014. Here, in *I am KEVIN! not Lewy* Kevin continues sharing his journey with Lewy Body Dementia that he started in his first book, *Lewy Body Dementia, Survival and Me*[2].

Lewy Body Dementia is one of a group of brain disorders that fall under the rubric, 'neurodegenerative disorders', of which Alzheimer's disease is the most common. Curiously, although most people have never heard of Lewy Body Dementia, it is the second most common form of progressive dementia, or, as is sometimes described, 'the most common form of dementia no one has ever heard of'. Lewy Body Dementia is caused by collections of abnormally

---

[1] Schneider Williams, Susan. *The terrorist inside my husband's brain*. *Neurology*. September 2015. **87** (13): 1308–1311.
[2] Quaid K. *Lewy Body Dementia Survival and Me*. June 2018

folded proteins (called Lewy bodies) which collect in critical areas of the brain, disrupting neuronal function and causing symptoms as perplexing as visual hallucinations, frightening nightmares, tremors and stiffness, impaired thinking and memory, and episodes of confusion.

*I am KEVIN! not Lewy* is a story of giving. The deep generosity that characterises Kevin Quaid comes through in every chapter of the book. He started his discovery mission to inform himself about his diagnosis, but from the outset, quickly found a platform to share his new-found knowledge with others, raising awareness of dementia, and, more particularly, Lewy Body Dementia. He does this first through his newly discovered talent for writing, sharing weekly columns with local newspapers. This soon transformed into sharing his views and knowledge through stakeholder panels, nationally and internationally, and now, through leading Ireland's first third sector organization to support people with Lewy bodies and their families, Lewy Body Ireland.

Finally, *I am KEVIN! not Lewy* is also a story of transition. The transition of Kevin and his wife, Helena, who once considered themselves simply man and wife, but, following Kevin's diagnosis of this life-changing condition, were transformed within the space of an hour to patient and caregiver. In an editorial I wrote in 2017 about the diagnosis of Parkinson's-related dementia, the group of conditions under which Lewy Body Dementia falls, I debated the merits of a diagnostic labelling. The editorial, entitled: *'Disrupted identities: Movement, mind, and memory in Parkinson's disease'*[3], cautioned against the ever-present risk of an enduring illness subsuming an individual's identity. Clinicians often fall into the trap of assuming the illness is the person and that the disease label defines their identity. In Kevin's description of his life with Helena following the diagnosis, we see how health and disease can impact identity, particularly when the disease can affect both body and mind, like Lewy Body Dementia. However, while Lewy Body Dementia has significantly shaped Kevin and Helena's life together, they have not allowed it to overwhelm them. *I am KEVIN! not Lewy* reveals Kevin's further transition from 'patient' to 'spokesperson', 'advocate', 'mentor', and 'expert stakeholder', with all the empowerment that these new labels embody. No 'tattered coat upon a stick', through his words and advocacy, Kevin Quaid sings his message, giving hope to all the other people around the world, *I am KEVIN! not Lewy*.

---

[3] Leroi, Iracema. *Disrupted identities: movement, mind, and memory in Parkinson's disease*. International Psychogeriatrics · June 2017 DOI: 10.1017/S1041610217000370

*Iracema Leroi, MD, FRCPC, MRCPsych*
*Associate Professor of Psychiatry*
*Global Brain Health Institute, Trinity College*
*Dublin*

*I used to think that the worst thing in life was to end up alone.*

*It's not.*

*The worst thing in life is to end up with people who make you feel alone.*

Robin Williams

# PROLOGUE

Robin Williams once wrote, 'I want to help people be less afraid.'[1] They are some of the most powerful words that I have ever heard since being diagnosed with Lewy Body Dementia (LBD).

Throughout this book, you will see that I make several references to Robin Williams and his name appears in the writing of other people who have contributed to this book. Robin's words are not the title of this book, but they could be, as it describes exactly what I want the book to do and it's how I want people to feel after reading it. My hope for you and your loved one is that by the end of this book, you will say to yourself, 'If they can do it, then so can I.'

During a radio interview with Karen Meenan *(Near FM 90.3)*, which included my wife, Helena, Professor Ian Mc Keith, a world-renowned expert on LBD from the UK, and Tylor Norwood, who directed the film *Robin's Wish*; we were all asked to pick a favourite poem to recite. Following is my poem, which I wrote, and it describes the way that Lewy Body Dementia took Robin Williams.

---

[1] *Robin's Wish*, directed by Tylor Norwood (2020, Vertical Entertainment)

# Kevin, Lewy and Robin

By Kevin Quaid

*Kevin knew Robin*

*Robin didn't know Kevin*

*Kevin made hundreds laugh*

*Robin made millions laugh*

*Laughter and good humour hid the pain*

*That Lewy was causing, again and again*

*Robin was in pain, but didn't know why*

*Kevin's pain was relentless*

*To the point that he would cry*

*Robin searched for answers*

*But couldn't find them*

*Kevin's search brought him Lewy*

*But he didn't let it define him*

*Lewy was the cause of the pain*

*Lewy was the cause of the fear*

*While draining us of our good cheer*


*Lewy was the reason Kevin and Robin hated the night*

*Lewy was the reason Kevin and Robin were consumed with fright*

*Lewy will make you think you are going mad and*

*Makes you forget the good times that you had*


*Lewy will hide and drive you insane*

*Lewy can cause you a world of pain.*

*Lewy is sneaky, menacing and unfair*

*Lewy Body Dementia just doesn't care.*

*Lewy took Robin without Robin knowing*

*Lewy tries to take Kevin, but Kevin is not for going.*


*Many a battle is had with Lewy*

*Some are won, some are lost*

*The end result is that it will cost,*

*Your body, your mind, and even your life*

*Unless you fight with all your might*


*Lewy Body Dementia is a horrible disease*

*It must be stopped and brought to its knees*

*So, join me in the fight*

*Bring it out to the light*

*Get rid of the stigma*

*Let's fight in plain sight.*


I hope that you enjoyed the poem and I hope that you enjoy my book.

*Life is what you make it*

*Live one day at a time*

*Live each day as if it's your last*

# Chapter 1

## LIFE CAN BE WHAT YOU MAKE IT

After writing my first book, **_Lewy Body Dementia, Survival and Me_**, in my wildest dreams I couldn't have imagined the results it would bring and the amount of people who have told me that it helped them change their lives. Not only people in Ireland; but in America, England, Holland, Germany, and Australia. I'm amazed at the number of emails that I have received from individuals thanking me for writing the book and, I admit, it feels good to know that you have helped someone. I also could not have imagined the number of wonderful people who have come into my life, and I have made lifelong friends, who now feel like family.

That is why I have decided to write this book, aimed at giving you hope. I want you to know that just because you or a loved one have been diagnosed with this horrible disease (or indeed any disease) it's not the end of the world.

For those who have been diagnosed with early onset LBD (like myself), and who may wonder if that's it, my life is over, what will I do now? Well, I am here to tell you that there is life out there after a diagnosis of Lewy Body Dementia. The reason I know this is because I have the lived experience and my wife, Helena, and I are living proof.

Like every situation following diagnosis with a serious illness, the affected person and their family can be thrown into a tailspin, and it can take some getting used to. As was our case when we visited the neurologist, and I was told that I had Lewy Body Dementia. (This following an earlier diagnosis of Parkinson's Disease.) After finding out that LBD is progressive and incurable, not only did we leave the neurologist's office as husband and wife (we now had two new titles). I was the patient and my wife, Helena, was my spousal caregiver.

Everyone who starts a new job will get some form of training and time to settle in, but not a caregiver. They are literally thrown in at the deep end. A lot to take in and a lot to process, and it took a while for everything to fall into place. And, while it was, we made plenty of mistakes.

Now, I will try to point you in the right direction by telling you some of our mistakes.

When I was first diagnosed, we told our family and friends and watched their shock. To them, I looked fine, and my memory didn't seem to be too bad, but at the same time, they knew there was something wrong with me, but dementia was the last thing on their minds. When it began to settle with them that I had a type of dementia that little it in 2017. I can tell you for the most part that the changes have been positive. There have been a few pitfalls and a hell of a lot of scary nights, but by-in-large, things have improved in my life and especially in my quality of life. Please don't think that my disease is improving because I can see its progression. But thank God, it's at a slower rate than I had first imagined, so I refuse to give up and I keep myself busy.

It pretty much starts with the kind of general practitioner (GP) you have and the information they give you. For me, I've been lucky to have such a wonderful GP and a wonderful team led by a brilliant neurologist.

When you are first diagnosed, it's very important to know what to do next and where to turn to, because there is help out there and wonderful people who are in the same position as yourself. I have met people in similar positions, some in a worse position, and indeed, others in a better position than myself. All these people have in a way become a big part of what I like to call my new family.

My new family came to be when my GP told me about our local dementia advisor, Amy Murphy. Such a dramatic change began the day she came into our lives.

We first met Amy in a place called the Memory Room in Mallow in County Cork and, luckily enough for me, it's only about a twenty-minute drive from our home. In the Memory Room there is an array of wonderful gadgets, simple but wonderful, to make the life of the person with dementia easier. (I will talk more about these gadgets in a later chapter and let you know some of the things that are there to help.)

That day, our discussion started with having a cup of coffee and Amy proceeded to tell Helena and me about some of the services that were available and the different social events that happen to suit people with dementia. She also told us about a wonderful organization here in Ireland, The Alzheimer Society of Ireland. (If you want to contact them, they have a Freephone number which is 1800 341 341.)

They are an organization, not just there to help people with Alzheimer's, but people with all types of dementia, their carers and their families. It's there that I really got to meet my new family and friends, and they enrich both our lives. Since then, we have become advocates for them and for people everywhere with dementia and their carers.

With our advocacy work, we have travelled all over Ireland and parts of Europe and it's fair to say that we have had our share of tears and laughter, and isn't that exactly what happens in families? You laugh together and you cry together. The

Alzheimer Society of Ireland has, without a doubt, saved my life and my sanity and, to be honest, has given me so much to look forward to on a weekly and monthly basis.

It's important in life to have something to look forward to and it's also important in life to have goals. I like to have short, medium and long-term goals, but I don't always achieve every one that I set. It's like any game, you might have a few shots at goal and miss every now and then and that is ok as well. I heard a saying once that 'it's not the destination that's important, but the journey' and how true that is. How many of us plan a trip and cannot wait to get there only to miss out on the excitement of the looking forward to the event and looking at all the good things and the fun that can be had along the way - along the journey? For me, that's the way my life has become. It's the journey that I am on, and, for me, the destination is nothing to look forward to, but, by God, I intend to enjoy the journey.

As I am writing this section of the book, I am in the train on my way to Dublin for a meeting with other members of The Alzheimer Society of Ireland. A journey that takes about two hours. Here is a massive change for me in the last twelve months, not that I am taking the train, but that I am on the train on my own. I am going to meet with other members of our Dementia Working Group and we are going to meet with a major company in Ireland who wants to become more dementia inclusive. (This is another subject that I will go into in more detail in later chapters.) The big thing for me is that I am no longer afraid to take a trip on my own. Don't get me wrong, I absolutely love when Helena accompanies me on my trips, but every now and then it's great to get away on my own and I am sure that my wife loves the break from me as well. As I speak, she is probably out tending to our beautiful rose garden.

As I have said about enjoying a journey on days like today, I sometimes use the time to write. On other days, I might just sit back with a cup of coffee and look out the window and enjoy as they say, 'the simple things in life'. I love looking at hay or silage being made and every couple of kilometres brings something new in the ever-changing landscape. It also gives me time to reflect on the past couple of days and I can often be seen on the Cork to Dublin train daydreaming and that is ok to do as well.

I have found that the more I use my brain the better my life can be and even though there is damage to my brain caused by the Lewy bodies, it doesn't define who I am or what I can do. My brain is like any other organ in the body, if I don't use it, I just might lose it. If you sit or lie down all the time and never move your legs, eventually you will not be able to walk, because your muscles will waste away from not being used. Well, I look at my brain in the same way and while I am able to use it, then that's what I intend to do.

Surrounding myself with very good friends outside of my new family has also been of tremendous help to me. Like everything in life, it's good to have a balance and, to be honest, I don't think that I ever really had a proper balance in my life until the year 2019. I have reached a point where I look at my advocacy work as my job, a job that I love with all my heart. But, when I am out having a pint, I feel like one of the boys, not Kevin Quaid who has Lewy Body Dementia, but Kevin Quaid who is part of the community and who has a laugh and a joke with the people I meet.

I am still fighting to get rid of the stigma that surrounds dementia and people with dementia, but believe it or not, where I come from everyone knows who I am and that I have dementia and they treat me no different than anybody else. If anything, letting people know that I have dementia has made my life so much easier and, not just my life, but Helena's as well. To share her insight, Helena has written a chapter in this book about what her life as my caregiver has been like in the last number of years.

My hope for you in this book is that you can form a picture for yourself from all the different things that have helped us as a family dealing with this horrible disease called Lewy Body Dementia.

This is a book of hope and don't for a minute be fooled into thinking that there is going to be a happy ending to the story. You will see my life laid out before you in as honest and accurate a way as possible with all its twists and turns. I once again have written the book myself, because I want it to be my story in my own words and the way that I tell it is as if you were sitting down next to me. I hope you enjoy it, but most of all, I hope it's helpful to you.

Since my diagnosis and because of my diagnosis, so many different people have come into my life, and I have travelled to so many different places. I want to show you what is possible for you. Yes, you the person reading this book if you have been diagnosed with LBD or if you are the caregiver. Dementia may eventually win the war, but I can promise you that you can win a lot of the battles along the way. This book is not all about living a happy and fun-filled life. It's about hope and about giving you hope when you have been diagnosed with a disease like dementia.

Please don't give up. Have a look at what your new life might bring you and look for the areas that could make your life a little easier, even a little happier.

# Chapter 2

# 12 SYMPTOMS

Here I have written a piece about the different symptoms of Lewy Body Dementia, and like all different types of dementias, symptoms may vary from one person to the next and it can also depend on how far along your journey with Lewy Body Dementia that you actually are.

This week I will focus on the type of dementia that I have, and it's called Lewy Body Dementia. The twelve signs that are associated with this type are: *DEMENTIA, HALLUCINATIONS, COGNITIVE FLUCTUATIONS, MOVEMENT DISORDER, POOR REGULATION OF BODILY FUNCTIONS, SLEEP PROBLEMS, DEPRESSION, APATHY, ANXIETY, AGITATION, DELUSIONS and PARANOIA.*

Keeping in mind what I said last week, 'when you meet one person with dementia you have met one person with dementia', meaning that no two people having been diagnosed with dementia will have or show the exact same symptoms and for this article I am talking only about myself and how this disease affects me.

### Dementia

This is the umbrella term used for all types of dementia, but when people hear the word, they assume that it's all about memory problems. For me and many other diagnosed with Lewy Body Dementia, it's not.

The memory problems that tend to bother me most are forgetting what I would have said or done five minutes ago, or it might take a while for me to recall what happened yesterday. The worst part for me, and it's getting worse lately, is when I awake in the mornings there are days that I cannot remember who I am, where I am or what day of the week it is. I find it is happening now more and more, and, in fact, it now happens to me most mornings and it can take me some time to figure out what's what and who I am?

### Hallucinations

I have gone into detail about the hallucinations in my book, **Lewy Body Dementia, Survival and Me**, but just to say I find them very frightening, and they can happen at any time... day or night.

Where they are particularly dangerous is if I'm a front seat passenger in a car and we come to a crossroads. The normal reaction of a driver is to say... 'Are we all right there?' But my response nowadays is... 'Have a look yourself because I can't be sure if there is a car coming or not.'

That's how real the hallucinations are when I experience them, in that I cannot tell the difference... what is real and what is imaginary?

It's the same when I see people. I never know if they are really there or not. That, for me, was the main reason for not driving anymore. Also, I sometimes have auditory hallucinations when I hear sounds and voices and these voices can be terrifying.

### Cognitive fluctuations

I suppose these cognitive fluctuations have more to do with the memory problems that I was talking about earlier. Some days my memory is perfect, but other days not so good.

For example, I could be on the phone to someone and finish the call, then thirty seconds later not even remember who I was talking to or what the conversation was about. Another example is when I'm having a conversation and especially if I'm making a point about something, I can be in the middle of the sentence and what I was trying to say or the point I was trying to make will go completely out of my head. Sometimes, it will not come back and, as I do a lot of public speaking, it has actually happened on a number of occasions and can be both annoying and embarrassing.

### Movement disorder

This movement disorder has been a problem for me for the last couple of years, and even though I now walk with the aid of a walking stick, I am grateful, because twelve months ago I could only walk with the aid of a walking frame.

Lewy Body Dementia can affect the way I walk. At times, I lose my balance for no reason, or I might have pain in my right hip today, my left hip tomorrow, my back the day after, and then might be OK the day after that. Sometimes, I can walk fine and, more times, it is only a slow shuffle. No two days are the same, that's for sure.

### *Poor regulation of bodily functions*

For me, this is a problem I don't think I will ever get used to and it more or less speaks for itself... poor regulation.

One of the big problems with a person who suffers from Lewy Body Dementia is getting infections of the urinary system including the urinary tract, bladder and kidneys. I have had kidney infections and if they go untreated can be very serious indeed. Sometimes, you can have a bad infection and not even know it.

What I find hard to deal with is if I am out for a few drinks, I could find myself using the bathroom at least every ten minutes, never able to completely empty the bladder. It's also important that I eat a healthy diet so that I can remain regular. On my last visit to my neurologist, I was told that my autonomic nervous system was affected and basically that means that the kidneys and other organs that regulate my bodily functions are not receiving the proper signals from my brain. (I do hope I am not ruining your breakfast by mentioning this... sorry!)

In many LBD sufferers, because the brain signals are interrupted, it could mean that their blood pressure can swing dangerously high or plummet extremely low or even have an irregular heart rhythm. They can experience prolonged hot flashes or frequent chills because their bodies cannot regulate hot or cold. These symptoms can happen without warning.

### Sleep problems

I have a complete chapter dedicated to this in my book, but for me, the nights are the worst. I find these sleep problems the biggest struggle of all with this disease. It's either insomnia and total fear of the 'dead of night', or I fall asleep and have terrible nightmares that are so real it's almost like living two separate lives. As I have said on many occasions, a good night is a night when I have a bad dream.

Others can experience a sleep problem called REM sleep behaviour disorder (RBD). With RBD, you aren't paralyzed during the REM stage. Instead, your body and voice act out your dreams while you remain asleep. So, if you are running and jumping in your dream, you might jump out of bed and have a serious fall. Or, if you are in the midst of a fist fight, you might punch your bed mate and cause them harm. This can be a serious concern and should not be ignored.

## Depression

Depression is one area that shows that people who have Lewy Body Dementia can vary greatly in.

I had been diagnosed with depression and placed on antidepressant tablets for a while, but I was taken off them last February and told by a consultant that I didn't have depression. For me to be told that was such a relief. Of course, there are days when I feel down and worry about the future and worry about what way I am going to end up, but I wonder if most people worry about the future anyway?

## Apathy

This is very real and can be a battle. Sometimes it feels like the easy thing to do is to stay at home and not go outside the door, and of course, there are days when I do not leave the house as it's my 'safe place'.

A big positive in my life is that I'm blessed with a wonderful wife who, in her own quiet way, will make sure that it does not happen very often and encourages me to get up and go when family and friends call to take me out. I admit, there are times that I have to push myself but, so far, I seem to be doing OK.

### Anxiety

'Anxiety is a natural reaction to threats or fears. These could be real or imagined.'[5] I can see where this can be a big problem and I can see how easily it could take over my life... IF I LET IT!

The way I deal with anxiety is to try and keep myself busy. I've gotten involved with The Alzheimer Society of Ireland (telephone number: 1800 341 341), who are a wonderful group of people who you can meet up with and we all help one another. Of course, there are days that I get anxious, but when I find it coming on, I try to do something, and I am so lucky to have such a wonderful family, friends and neighbours.

For others, if you don't feel you can relieve the anxiety in some way by yourself, then you should speak to your health consultant.

### Agitation

Agitation is a mix of anxiety and restlessness. When a person with dementia feels agitated, they cannot rest or stay still. They feel they have to move. At these times it can be hard for a person to understand what's happening to them, and it can become difficult to deal with. Agitation feels awful and can have a negative effect on every aspect of their life.[6]

---

[5] *Agitation and Frustration.* The Alzheimer Society of Ireland. Factsheet B4. September 2020

There are days that I get very agitated and very angry and maybe have a bit of self- pity. The days that affect me most are the days when I feel like doing a few jobs around the house or garden, and I go out with great intentions only to find myself back on the couch exhausted after maybe only half an hour. This really frustrates me a lot.

### Delusions

Delusions are false beliefs. For example, a person with dementia might believe that workers in a nursing home are poisoning meals or stealing. Delusions can be frustrating and difficult to deal with because they affect how someone with dementia relates to others.[7]

I can, at times, let my imagination run away with me but for the most part I can stop and bring myself back to reality. Most others have no insight into their delusions and cannot be convinced that their reality is fictional, so it's left up to the carer to learn strategies on how to respond to these events.

Hopefully I can continue to be somewhat aware and rational for some time to come yet.

---

[6] *Agitation and Frustration.* The Alzheimer Society of Ireland. Factsheet B4. September 2020

[7] *Causes of Hallucinations & Delusions in Dementia and Caregiver Tips for Coping.* May 2020.
https://www.dementiacarecentral.com/caregiverinfo/hallucinations-and-delusions/

### Paranoia

WebMD© describes paranoia as 'the feeling that you're being threatened in some way'. This could be an uneasy sensation as if you're being watched by other people, or that someone is out to get you. These feelings (in order for it to be justified as paranoia) are not based on any evidence.[8]

Every now and again I do get a little paranoid about things but, for me, it wouldn't be my biggest problem.

*Kevin Quaid, 2019, The Vale Star*
*(Updated 2021)*

---

[8] Georgina, Chanel. *Dementia symptoms: Paranoia may be a sign of the debilitating condition.* https://express.co.uk December 2020.

*A symphony of symptoms*

*Better or worse?*

*Not all scars show*

*Not all wounds heal*

*Not all illnesses can be seen*

*Not all pain is obvious*

*Please remember this before you judge someone*

## Chapter 3

# A SYMPHONY OF SYMPTOMS... BETTER OR WORSE

As I said at the beginning, I want this book to be a positive one. It's not going to be filled with false hope but of real life and real living, and you will see the highs and lows that I have gone through as a result of LBD.

In Chapter 12 of my last book, **Lewy Body Dementia, Survival and Me**, I went through a list of symptoms that I had at the time. Now, a couple of years later, I want to go through each and every one to see if there has been any change in them. If so, was the change good or bad or was there any change at all. So, for those of you that haven't read my first book, I will list each one and underneath, tell you how I am doing now, what is different, and what I have done to improve the situation.

As I mentioned in my first book, April 2017 was a particularly bad time for me. Before a visit with my neurologist, I prepared a list of symptoms so that I could let him know the details. Here's the list of things that bothered me the most at that time.

### Hip pain

I seemed to have constant pain especially in my right hip and sometimes radiating across my back and into my left hip.

I had been diagnosed with Paget's Disease[9] in Australia after having a nuclear medicine scan. They told me that Paget's was the cause of my hip pain and that explained those symptoms. However, the specialist in Ireland, following on from other scans, believed that because the pain I had was so severe, he didn't believe that Paget's was responsible. Two doctors, two countries and two different opinions.

At that time, I was walking with the use of a walking frame, and it was around then that I was put on Butrans® patches, gradually increasing to 30 mg. I stayed on them until January 2018.

---

[9] Paget's Disease of bone disrupts the normal cycle of bone renewal, causing bones to become weakened and possibly deformed. https://www.nhs.uk/conditions/pagets-disease-bone/

sometimes not. There are times when Helena might point it out to me saying, 'You must be feeling bad this morning because I notice it in your speech.' To be honest, it sometimes feels very embarrassing, especially if I am talking to someone who wouldn't have heard me speak that way before. I do find, however, that my speech will return to normal within fifteen to twenty minutes.

**Difference now**

This can still happen and especially if I find myself getting tired. Helena says that some evenings she can see me wilting and then it happens. It can also happen if I get an infection and I am put on a lot of medication. I have had some infections, which I will go into in more detail later in the book, but it has only happened on a few occasions where the medication has affected my speech.

So, the slurred speech has definitely improved and, again, I put that down to the CBD oil and the aloe vera juice. I want to point out very clearly that this is what I do and what works for me. I am in no way saying that it will work for everyone... Result: Positive!

**Handwriting**

My handwriting was never very exact or too perfect, and I even remember at National School spending extra time on perfecting my writing skills.

The best way for me to explain it, is that I couldn't write a clear letter A, E or O.  There would always be a line or part of a line through it. My handwriting could be read quite easily, and it was never a problem as far as exams or work was concerned, but now it's different.

As I write, I go from big to small letters, very stretched out, and from joined up writing to printing. I find that it takes extra concentration to write any more than a few words, and it has now gone to the stage where I can't even read my own writing after a couple of days. It's something that I have pretty much given up on and, as I need to keep a small diary with me at all times, I now just put words rather than sentences in it.

### Difference now

As I have pointed out, and it's been clearly pointed out to me, my handwriting was never good anyway and for 99% of my writing I use my laptop anyway. So, I have to say that it has not gotten any better or worse.  The amazing thing is that I can draw a clock again with the time on it, which was part of a test I completed when I was first diagnosed with Parkinson's. I can also draw a cube, now, so I am delighted to say... Result: Positive!

### Sudden sweating

This happens to me for no apparent reason. I just start to sweat so badly that my shirt gets wet and my forehead, also. Thankfully, within a couple of minutes, my temperature returns to normal. I suppose I could describe it as a car just overheating for a few minutes and then back to normal again.

These episodes of sudden sweating don't happen with any great frequency, nor can I say at any specific time. They occur out of the blue maybe every day for five days and then may not happen again for a week or two. The only good thing about it is that it goes as quickly as it comes.

### Difference now

The difference now is quite remarkable. The sweating only happens to me now when in bed and only on the rare occasion. It normally only happens as the result of a bad nightmare, but sometimes it can be a warning sign that I am getting an infection. So, I have to say... Result: Positive!

### Confusion

I have noticed that my confusion is getting worse. I can now just be introduced to someone and within a couple of minutes, I have forgotten their name. What's more disturbing for me is when family names are a problem for me. All too often, nowadays, I get confused but when told their name, I'm good again. I can also be a little confused about what day, date, or what year it is.

## Difference now

Unfortunately, confusion is one area of my life that has not gotten any better and, to be honest, has gotten worse over time. (The only good thing is that it is gradually happening.) I am very aware when it happens as it is frightening when I get confused or overwhelmed by even something small. Let me give you one example…

I haven't driven for a few years because of visual hallucinations; therefore, I don't have anything to do with getting the car serviced, etc. Recently, after a very frosty night, the car would not start for Helena. I was so surprised at how confused I was about what she should do that I actually got frightened to the point where I felt sick in my stomach. I then cannot understand why such a small thing can confuse me to such a degree and I have to remind myself that it's not me that's the problem, it's the Lewy bodies in my brain… Result: Negative!

*Tremors*

I presented with tremors in my left hand and right leg. I had noticed them for a long time, maybe even six months before I had ever gone to the neurologist. I am left-handed, (a 'Ciotóg' as we say in Ireland) therefore, when this tremor developed in my left hand, at first, I found it to be more of a nuisance than anything else. Unfortunately, it worsened over time and got so bad that I couldn't hold a glass or a cup because I would spill everything.

Sometimes, the tremor in my left hand does not seem too bad, but maybe it's because the focus is off of it. I'm thinking it's because my right leg would just start to shake when I was lying down (it's considered a resting tremor) and I found it very noticeable if I was lying on the couch watching TV. This could continue for hours, but now it has gotten to the stage where I really don't take much notice of it anymore. I don't let it bother me.

On occasion, I also have a tremor in my left leg, but not as often as my right. The worst time for me is in the morning, and especially if I have to get up within minutes of waking up. It's important for me to have at least 15 to 20 minutes or sometimes longer as a transition period between waking and getting out of bed. It gives me time to get my bearings, almost like getting off a boat with the sea legs still intact. If when I wake up, I just lay in bed for a little while, then I can get out of bed with no problems as such. But, if I get out of bed within the first five minutes, I will find it very hard to get my balance. There are times when it feels like my whole body is trembling and it can be quite frightening because this feeling can last up to ten to fifteen minutes.

With this trembling comes slurred speech and I just don't feel right. The thought sometimes enters my head, 'My God, what happens if this feeling doesn't stop? Is this it?' If I'm not careful, I could work myself into a bit of a panic attack quite easily. The best way I find to counteract it, is to just try to ignore it and reassure myself that it will pass in a couple of minutes. I do believe that you can send the strongest message to your mind from yourself while being assertive about it. *'This will get better... This too shall pass.'*

### Difference now

The change in me is simply massive and in a good way.

Now, I'm very glad to say that I have trained myself to use my right hand, so I don't notice the can go for days and survive on just a small meal. There is no actual pattern to it.

I have also found that when I feel hungry and while thinking of what I might eat, I can go right off of the idea. This is especially obvious in the mornings. I would say to myself that I would like a boiled egg and toast, for example, and by the time I get to the kitchen, I find myself forcing down just a cup of tea. I try as best I can to have breakfast, dinner and supper but, to be honest, I only succeed maybe two or three days a week. The rest is very mixed up. Sometimes, I might have one big meal before going to bed, and some days, I might have no proper meal.

### Difference now

As far as my food is concerned, I have made some changes.

Some of the biggest changes I've made include becoming a lot more consistent with the times that I eat, being very conscious of what I eat, and eating smaller portions. As I am trying to lose weight, I have gotten the help of a dietitian and, so far, all is good. As with everything in life, it's good to have a routine and a bit of discipline.

I have always said that your breakfast is the most important meal of the day and now I make a habit of having a breakfast every morning. I vary it every day and that seems to take away a lot of the cravings that I used to have. So as far as my eating habits and my food intake is concerned, I am very happy. I am no saint, but I do try, and, of course, enjoying a treat every now and then is good... Result: Positive!

### Loud noise

Ever since I was a little boy, I hated loud noises or sudden bangs. For instance, a car backfiring, frightened me then and still does to this day.

In the last few years, the biggest things that I have noticed bother me, are people talking loudly or crowds of people talking. I have said to Helena on several occasions when visitors are calling, 'Why is everyone shouting?' There are even times when I will leave the room as I just cannot stand the loud noise.

The same can be said of crowds. I will try as best I can to avoid places with crowds, especially family gatherings or where a lot of people want to talk to me. I now find situations like this overwhelming. Maybe not all of the time, but a lot of the time. Again, if possible, I will avoid the situation.

Even if someone pops a piece of bubble-gum close to me, it hurts my head, so I have found that putting in my earphones and listening to music is a great comfort.

Funny, the one thing I find worse than loud noises or crowds is complete silence. When there is complete silence and calm, I can hear almost a constant buzzing in my brain. It is very faint, but it's always there and that is as bad as any noise. I get the feeling that I am going mad and, again, it calls for me to be strong and tell myself that I will be able to get out of the situation and fix it. It might be as simple as putting on the TV or radio in the background. For me, nowadays, complete silence is out of the question. Again, it's a question of finding a sort of happy medium.

### Difference now

I could write the very same piece again as I still feel exactly the same. For me, when something is not getting worse then that can only be a good thing. The fact that the family knows about my noise sensitivity is such a help because if there are more than four people in our house, I will normally go into a different room. I can still have conversations with people, but not in large or especially noisy groups. Not all the time, but sometimes… Result: Positive!

**Other symptoms:**

### *Diverticulitis*

I had a colonoscopy done in 2016 which showed that I had diverticulitis, which is inflammation or infection of pouches that can form in the intestines, and which I still have to this day. There are times when I get a flare up and when it does, I feel pretty awful, but then I can have a period when it settles down and all is OK.

### *Difference now*

This is one of those things that I can pretty much control myself and I can safely say that since I started to drink aloe vera juice on a daily basis, I have not had a flare up. The only time that I might have a flare up is if I am on strong medication for an infection, but I just increase my intake of aloe vera juice… Result: Positive!

### *Asthma*

I was diagnosed with asthma in 2016 having spent a few days in hospital in Mallow with chest pain. I also have sleep apnoea and I use the sleep apnoea machine whenever I sleep and find it very helpful. I will go into this in more detail later on.

### Difference now

I only feel the need for my inhalers once or twice a month, which is simply a huge change. Occasionally, I may need to use it twice a day, but I think a lot depends on the weather, as well as my sleep apnoea machine, which I use every night.

In addition to the apnoea machine, which is a brilliant comfort to me, not being on as much medication, I also feel has been of enormous help. I don't think that I could go to sleep now without my sleep apnoea machine and, even if we go away for a night, I take the machine with me… Result: Positive!

### Energy levels

A few weeks ago, my energy levels were at an all-time low, but I have to say that with a change in lifestyle, a daily routine, and some light exercise, such as going for a short walk, they seem to be on the up again. Like everything in my life now, I have good days and bad days, but I'm beginning to see that the more structure I have in my day, the better my energy levels seem to be.

### Difference now

As I said earlier, I can do little bits of jobs around the house and, compared to the way I was, my energy levels have increased 150%. Now, don't get me wrong, I am far from running a marathon and never will get there, but I feel, once again, there has been a remarkable improvement in this area of my life. Once a person knows their limits and sticks to them, then everything will fall into place... Result: Positive!

As I said, these were pretty much the symptoms that I presented with on my second trip to see my neurologist in Cork in early 2017, and this is where I am as I write in the middle of 2020.

By the time you are reading this book, it will be later, and out of thirteen different areas of my life, and the things that have and do still affect me, eleven of them are heading in a positive direction and only two in a negative direction.

If you had told me that this would be the case when I was first diagnosed, I probably would not have believed you, but as you continue to read this book you will see that the way I live my life now and my positive frame of mind have led me to get such positive results. My Lewy Body Dementia is, as I have said progressing, but so is my determination not to let it get the better of me for as long as I possibly can.

As everyone knows, writing a book can take a long time and I want to let you know how I am feeling today. This is the 7th of April 2021, still in the COVID-19 lockdown, and, as you will see throughout the book, I keep myself very busy with my advocacy work and my writing and that keeps my brain active. I am happy with the way my brain is still coping with everyday life and, again, I am lucky with the people that I have around me.

On a physical level, I am currently being treated for a bladder problem and because people who live with Lewy Body Dementia can be very sensitive to different types of medication, it's of vital importance that the dose of medication you receive is small and then you can work your way up to the recommended dose. Know that this is a conversation you need to have with your GP, and IT MIGHT DO NO HARM TO REMIND HIM/HER.

Some time ago, I walked with the aid of a walking stick, but then, unfortunately, had to rely on the use of a walking frame, and while I didn't like it, I had to get used to it. My walking was so bad that we had to get some of our house modified, so wheelchairs could fit out the different doors, as well as around the house. That's supposed to be the natural progression; you go from walking to a walking stick, to a walking frame, and then to a wheelchair.

Well, I am here to tell you, and as you probably know about me by now, I just don't go with the flow. I am back with my walking stick and to be honest, I keep it with me all the time and everywhere I go. I probably only need it 50% of the time, but then my balance will go, and I will fall, so the smart thing to do is to keep it with me all the time. I don't have to use it when I am inside my house because there is always a chair or a wall to fall up against or to use as a support. Instead of looking at my walking stick as an obstacle, I look at it as my friend who gives me my independence. I have a couple of sticks, but one has become my favourite. I find it amazing that something like a walking stick that I hated when I first started to use it, I now consider it as my friend.

When we were not in pandemic lockdown and I would go for a drive with a neighbour of mine, he would often be asked, 'Where is the fellow with the stick?' This has been said to me as well, 'Oh look, it's the man with the stick.' It's meant in a fun and kind way and not a mocking and condescending way. It's just another way of making sweet lemonade out of sour lemons.

*Putting new talents to good use*

*It's never too late to start again*

## Chapter 4

## PUTTING NEW TALENTS TO GOOD USE

When you read the last chapter, you could see that not all of my symptoms had gotten worse, indeed, some had even improved. Each week can bring different issues, and as they show up, I try and deal with them the best I can.

The answer for me, is keeping in touch with my medical team and staying on top of the problem, but more importantly, distraction helps, so I try to keep busy. I have already told you that I have a love for writing, which for me is a new skill, an addition rather than a loss, as Lewy has taken a lot.

Well, at least I think writing is a skill that I discovered since being diagnosed with Lewy Body Dementia, and it really didn't hit me until one of the first radio interviews I did. It was with one of my local radio stations here in Mallow, Cork's 103FM, hosted by the wonderful Patricia Messenger, and before she interviewed both Helena and I, she introduced me as 'Author' Kevin Quaid. I laughed at the idea because it was the first time that someone had actually called me an author, and as Patricia said to me, 'That's what you are now.' That gave me a massive lift and huge encouragement to keep going with this sort of work and see where it would take me. I had been called a lot of things in my life, but this was definitely a first.

Since then, I have been on her show a number of occasions, and she is another one of the wonderful people, who not only did I get to know, but who I am so proud to call my friend. I often put up a post on Twitter© and Patricia is always one of the first to congratulate or encourage me and that means so much.

In Chapter 1, I told you that I write for three local papers thanks to their editor, Mike Biggane, and for the next couple of chapters I would like to share some of the articles that mean a lot to me. Articles that people seem to like and to take a lot from, which for me, is what my writing is all about.

My first book, **Lewy Body Dementia, Survival and Me**, took me to places that I would have never imagined. For one, I will give you a sample of some of the media work that both Helena and I did as part of raising awareness and removing the stigma associated with dementia as a whole.

As part of this advocacy work, we were on one of Ireland's national radio stations and one of their most popular afternoon radio shows, 'The Ray D'Arcy Show'. We were first on with him to talk about my first book, which he had read, and told me that he loved. He helped to shine a light on our experience of living with Lewy Body Dementia and, especially from Helena's perspective, as my spousal caregiver. (If you are interested in the interview, it is available on podcast. Just look up 'Kevin Quaid' on 'Ray D'Arcy' on YouTube©.)

All the counties in Ireland have local radio stations. Another one that we were both on was Kerry Radio, on another very popular afternoon radio show called 'Talkabout' with the very beautiful Deidre Walsh.

I have been on her show on several occasions since and I am delighted to say that Deidre and we have become great friends and she constantly gives me great encouragement. The response from her first interview with us in County Kerry was incredible, and the hunger for knowledge, not only about dementia in general, but for Lewy Body Dementia, was unbelievable. The amount of people who wanted to hear from and about Helena and her life as a caregiver, was truly amazing.

Both Helena and I knew at this stage that our message about raising awareness on the hidden side of Lewy bodies was getting through, especially with local radio, as well as the national radio.

The 'Neil Prendeville Show' from Cork city was next to come calling. Neil has a large listenership, and again, the response to his show was amazing.

I suppose most people would like the chance to be on television, and so we were, upon being invited to be on RTÉ's (Ireland's National Public Service Media) very popular daytime show 'Today with Maura and Dáithí'. And, as you will also see later, I was on many different local radio stations and pretty much every paper in the country, all to carry on the fight to eliminate the stigma around dementia.

The story of my book and my life since I was diagnosed with Lewy Body Dementia, would have probably never have seen the light of day but for a lovely journalist who lives in my locality. I have to say a special word of thanks to a local Kanturk man by the name of Timmy Lynch who writes for **The Corkman Newspaper**, another local paper covering all of County Cork and online all over the world. It was Timmy who started the ball rolling with the first newspaper article and it was Timmy who organised my first radio interview with Patricia Messenger. Timmy is another man who I have become very friendly with, and we meet for a Guinness every now and then... 'Thank you, Timmy.'

I am not mentioning all of these names to brag, but to just show you some of the wonderful people and friends that I have met along the way.

# Chapter 5

# HOW'S MY FAVOURITE NEPHEW?

*Bereavement hits every family in the world and each and every one of us has experienced it. The natural order of things is that children will mourn the loss of their grandparents, parents, uncles and aunts, and so on, and that is the way that life is supposed to be. But all too often, it can happen the other way around, and that is very, very hard on people, especially parents who have to say goodbye to a child.*

The dedication at the start of the book mentions my lovely aunts and uncles, and highlights my uncle, Billy Norris. This is the piece that I wrote about him and about how I was feeling that particular week. I don't want to change any of it, because as you read each article, you will see how I was during that week and how I was feeling at the time of writing. Here is the article.

> This week there wasn't much going on, but I did find myself very tired and had a couple of bad nights. I got very little sleep some nights and there were more nights when I did sleep, that the dreams/nightmares were just horrible,

but that is part of Lewy Body Dementia. I put it down to the fact that the week before was very busy and at times I need to pace myself a little better. That's the thing with Lewy Body Dementia, when I feel good there are times that I push myself a little bit too much and then I feel the effects of it for days afterwards.

There was one day this week that really stands out for me, and it was the day that I got a phone call from my uncle, Billy Norris, and his wife, Joan, who I haven't spoken to in a while. The start of the phone call was as follows...

'How's my favourite nephew?' That is how my uncle has spoken to me as far back as I can remember. There's no hello, it's simply, 'How's my favourite nephew?' I don't want to make any of his other nephews and nieces jealous, only to say that we talked about long ago or, as they say, now back in the day. He reminded me that I used to call a wheelbarrow a 'BYGOR' when I was a little boy and we laughed; we reminisced and both of us wondered where the years have gone. The one thing I lovingly remember about this man, Uncle Billy... is that he always seems to be in good humour and whenever he is around you can be sure of a good laugh.

It got me thinking, while it's Lewy Body Dementia I have, and thankfully, my memory is still pretty good most of the time, I wonder if a person who is suffering from Alzheimer's feels like this when they recall a memory. I hope it takes them back to a wonderful time in their lives, to a time when they were happy. I started thinking about our phone call and how our conversation transported me to a time and place, as if what we had discussed only happened a couple of days before. The thing about dementia is that there are different stages and to keep it simple you basically have the early stages, the middle stages and the end stage. Unfortunately, the end stage is not nice for any one of us nor for the family looking on, but until then there is a lot that we can do.

The next time you are talking to your loved one and they seem a little confused or their memory is slipping, talk about something from their past, you may have to ask a couple of questions to get a conversation going, but once you do, just watch and listen to how the conversation will go and how happy your loved one will be to be part of it. I can bet you that the detail they will remember will amaze you, they might not remember who you are, or they may mix you up with someone else and that's OK.

I know of one lovely lady who thinks that her daughter is actually her sister, but when talking about the past, they seem to be so happy and content. Like I have said on several occasions, when the person with dementia is talking to you and not making sense to you... please remember that this is their reality, this is where they are now and, more often than not, this is what is making them happy. So, if it's not upsetting to them, go along with it and believe it or not, you might also like to be reminded of good times from the past. On the other hand, if your loved one is talking about something they don't like or something that is frightening to them, don't just correct them, instead try to reassure them and tell them that they are safe. Tell them that you are there, tell them that everything is OK and that everything will be OK.

At the later stages of dementia, people might not be able to respond or even talk, but just like people in a coma, don't just sit there looking at them, talk to them, remind them of how much they are loved, and maybe talk about a beautiful memory from the past.

If a person is what we call in the middle stages of dementia, there are a few small tips that may help you. When talking to your loved one only use small, short sentences, nothing too complicated; touch their hand, speak softly, look them in the eye, and above all, smile. If you are asked a question, make sure you listen and hear what is said.

I have said before that one of my aims is to start making my local town, Kanturk, a dementia-friendly town, and my journey starts this week when I visit Killaloe in County Clare, where they have started to make the town dementia-friendly. I was also delighted to see that Gatwick Airport in London has taken a big step in making their airport dementia-friendly, with special facilities and services such as: *A Special Assistant Brochure* to help you with your journey through the airport, and a Sensory Room, to name but two.

I hope we are beginning to turn the corner as far as the stigma is concerned and beginning to realise that dementia is organ failure and the organ is the brain. If we all do our own small little bit to help, then hopefully living with dementia will become a little bit easier for everyone involved, the people who live with this brain disease, as well as the people who support and care for them.

Being an advocate for a person living with dementia and being a supporter and carer of a person with dementia is an ongoing process, and if we keep talking about it and keep working at it and keep bringing it out in the open, then we can make the lives of the people who really matter just a little bit easier.

*Kevin Quaid, 2018, The Vale Star*
*(Updated 2021)*

## Chapter 6

## STAYING ACTIVE IS THE NAME OF THE GAME

I have spoken a lot about staying active and continuing to do the things you like doing. This is true for anybody who has dementia; indeed, it is true in most walks of life. I believe in following this old adage, 'find a job that you love, and you will never have to work a day in your life'.

Lewy Body Dementia, like most dementias that I know of, is 'progressive and incurable' (the words used by one of my consultants when discussing my diagnosis). I suppose when you hear these words first, well for me anyway, they didn't even register. But, when they do register, it's enough to make your blood run cold and you feel like going and hiding in the darkest corner you can find. Indeed, some poor people do curl up in darkness and who can blame them. When I finally came to terms with the fact that I have Lewy Body Dementia, I turned it around and made it a challenge.

I like to think that when I was thrown to the wolves (my wolf being Lewy Body Dementia), I came back as leader of the pack. Now, don't think for a moment that it's all good and I have conquered this horrible disease. In fact, two weeks ago it came back to remind me that it's still here and very much the boss. If my life with LBD was a boxing match, then two weeks ago it won the round with a three-day knockdown.

One of the problems with my Lewy Body Dementia can be infections. They can be stealthy, developing slowly and silently, and in my case, the likes of a kidney infection can be silent for a number of days and then bang... it hits you fair and square and that is exactly what happened.

I hadn't been feeling great on the Tuesday and went to the doctor that evening and was put on a course of strong antibiotics for 8 days. On Wednesday, I had a scheduled visit with my neurologist, and then by Friday, you could not understand a word I was saying.

What springs to mind is how one of my consultants in Cork told me that too much medication actually feeds Lewy Body Dementia and some medications can have a decidedly negative impact. In this case, however, I had no choice but to ramp up my medication 'till it won the battle' over the severe infection that I was dealing with. It was fair to say, as they say in Australia, 'I was fairly crook'. On the following Monday, I came good again just in time to return to my advocacy work with The Alzheimer Society of Ireland (ASI).

The ASI had both Helena and I booked to speak to a group in The Royal College of Surgeons (RCSI) in Dublin. The group consisted of medics from different disciplines who were about to take up their roles in various hospitals and some who were already working within the hospital system. The RCSI Hospital Group consists of Beaumont Hospital, Cavan & Monaghan Hospitals, Connolly Hospital, Louth County Hospital, Our Lady of Lourdes Hospital in Drogheda, and the Rotunda Hospital. As you can see from that list, there are a lot of hospitals that serve a large number of patients, and in the mix of that, many people who have, or who know someone who has, some type of dementia.

So, it's brilliant that from day one they wanted to hear from people who are directly affected by dementia and, not only the person with dementia, but also the carer. I will give you a flavour of what we spoke about as we endeavour to raise awareness about dementia in Ireland and especially raise awareness of Lewy Body Dementia as LBD is one type that is rarely addressed.

As always, I introduced myself, spoke about my family and then told them that I have Lewy Body

Dementia. The reason I tell everything about myself first and about LBD last, is to try and let people see that there is a lot more to a person than just their disease and that we should not be defined by it.

I continued on about how brilliant my medical team is and the importance of being able to talk to your doctor about anything, especially that you can and should be completely honest with your GP. I also said that it is of vital importance that the doctors listen to the patient and take on board what the patient has to say. I have had brilliant experiences with every doctor that I have seen, all except one, and I will not be meeting that doctor again. For me, it's important to have a friendly, yet professional, relationship with my doctors, and if I don't understand what they are saying or what they mean, I will ask them to explain it as they say 'in layman's terms'. There is nothing worse than leaving a doctor's surgery more confused than when you walked in. I explained to them, and as you have heard me say before, 'When you meet one person with dementia, you have met one person with dementia'. That simply means that no two people will be the same or have the exact same symptoms.

I went on to explain that dementia in all its forms is a family disease, in that it also affects your loved ones who see you suffering due to this life-changing diagnosis. Helena is a great advocate for carers and is a member of the Dementia Carers Campaign Network (DCCN). She speaks openly about living with LBD from her point of view; shares her experience, strength and hope around the journey of being a spousal carer, while raising awareness around 'carer burnout' and the many health issues that are attached if the carer is not attentive to their own needs.

As we have experienced at prior engagements, we got a fantastic response. So, it was another busy week and a week where I had to use my brain. This helps me to feel good and keep me active and for me now… that's what it's all about.

# Chapter 7

## TRAVELLING ALONE OR WITH A COMPANION ON IRISH RAIL

Getting out and about is an important part of life and of vital importance for everyone, and of course, it is a healthy thing to do.

I see for the likes of myself, that if I stay at home and indoors for any couple of days in a row, I get what I like to call, cabin fever. I know that for some people taking a journey can be a big task and especially for people who have a diagnosis of dementia, it can indeed be a frightening experience. But where does the fear come from?

I believe that it's a fear of the unknown, and, more than likely, completely unfounded. But, for the person who has it, it's as real as it gets. The most frightening thing is when you cannot put your finger on the fear, it makes it all the harder to understand. I will give you an example.

If you are afraid of dogs, and you come across a barking dog and are afraid that he may bite you, that's a fear that you can explain. The type of fear that I am talking about cannot be logically explained, but is every bit as bad, and sometimes worse, than that fear of the biting dog. Now, you are probably saying, 'What in the name of God has this got to do with a train journey?' Well, I will tell you.

When Helena and I started to do advocacy work for The Alzheimer Society of Ireland, we both started to attend frequent meetings in Dublin. As we live in Kanturk, we use the train from Mallow to Dublin, almost weekly. Other times, we will decide to go from Banteer, as it is only about 10 minutes from the house. But, more often, the reason that we travel from Mallow is because there is train service to Heuston station, Dublin, every hour. That is a brilliant service.

For my first couple of journeys, I wouldn't dream of travelling on my own due to the fear that I had. (As I said before, the fear of the unknown.) Now, a year and a half later, if Helena doesn't have a meeting on the same day, I have no problem hopping on a train in Mallow and going to Dublin or going anywhere for that matter.

The trick to a journey is simple, and here are a few simple steps that I follow.

1. Know where you are going
2. Know what time the trains are travelling
3. Know what time the trains are coming back
4. Write everything down
5. Ask for confirmation of everything at the station

I will go through each step with you.

1.  Know where you are going. Seems simple, but to a person with dementia this can be complicated. So, write it down!

    Also vitally important, check how much time you need to get to your destination, including the time to get to and from the station.

2.  As Irish Rail has such a brilliant service, check online or at your local station for the train times. Be aware, there are different timetables for the weekend, so your trip times for Monday to Friday will be different from Saturday and Sunday. A good tip is to have the train timetables at home.

    Again, allow yourself plenty of time to get to the station and allow yourself plenty of time to get to your destination at the other side.

    What I like to do is get to the train station about half an hour before the train is due to depart and get my ticket and a cup of coffee. Just to let you know... there is the most beautiful coffee available at the shop in Mallow train station.

3.  It seems simple, but to someone with dementia, it may not. Check the train times for your return journey and, again, allow yourself plenty of time for a cup of tea or coffee and to relax before departing.

4.  Have your notebook with you at all times and write everything down. Include the time your train is leaving, how many stops to your destination, whether you need to change trains at any of the stops, the time of your arrival, and what plans have you made for when you get to your destination.

    Once arrived, do you need to get a taxi or a bus? If you are using a taxi service, your taxi should be waiting for you near the train platform which is well signposted.

    Write the important times, etc. in your notebook for your return journey. Then when you are on the train, and you get a little confused, you can just get out your notebook, go through the steps you have written down, and that should help to alleviate any stress you may be under.

5.  When you are at the station, show the handwritten timetable of your intended journey to a member of the staff at Irish Rail and ask them to verify that your train times are correct. Also, ask them which platform your train will be leaving from, and any other related questions you may have.

    I have no problem telling the staff at any station that I have dementia. I have found that the staff at Irish Rail are some of the most caring and considerate people I have ever met. They are always willing to go that extra step to help you out.

Recently, I and other members of The Alzheimer Society of Ireland Irish Dementia Working Group, met with a team from Irish Rail for a number of meetings. These were held to assess how they can improve to make the journey for people with dementia easier and more pleasant.

Last week, we gave a walk around Heuston Station and had a look at some of the services that are already in place and how they can be improved upon. There are 'Help Points', and 'Emergency' and 'Assistant' buttons located throughout the station. Heuston Station has committed to making some massive improvements to areas like the toilets and are taking our input into consideration when making the necessary changes and value what we might like to see at their station.

Our working group is pleased to work with Irish Rail to improve train service for those with dementia, and, in turn, people with other illnesses and disabilities will also benefit.

The same can be said of the bus services here in Ireland. If at the train station and in the city, just ask a member of staff where the bus stop is to whatever area you want to go to. Then, when you get to the bus, the driver is always willing to help and to tell you which stop to get off at. Being from rural Ireland and travelling to a city like Dublin can be a very fearful and daunting task but having the knowledge that the bus driver will be of help in getting to your location can bring peace of mind. The same can be said of the interlink bus services between the different towns and cities. It gives peace of mind, and isn't that what you want, whether you have dementia or any other type of illness or disability?

For those of you that are handy with a computer, you can pre-book your train seats online. For those who prefer the one-to-one touch, you can telephone and pre-book your seat.

If you are nervous about your journey, you can also book assistance. That is when you contact them, express your fears or worries and they will have a staff member available to meet you at the door of your particular carriage and assist you to your seat. Remember, if you are worried at any stage of your journey, always ask a member of staff for assistance. They are brilliant people and really do care about their customers.

I recently went on a day trip to Killarney just to see what a short and local journey would be like. I travelled from Mallow to Killarney, and then from Killarney back to Banteer. When I arrived in Mallow, I had everything written down and went to the ticket desk to get my ticket. I explained that I had dementia and described the journey that I was about to take. I showed the friendly staff

We mentioned that we were starting to make Kanturk a dementia-friendly town and to kick-start that off, we were having an afternoon tea in Kanturk's Daily Grind Café, a beautiful coffee shop with a varied menu of gorgeous food and pastries. This would be held on the first Wednesday of every month starting on 6th March 2019.

I am delighted to tell you that it was an amazing success. We had people there who, for the first time ever, openly discussed their dementia diagnosis. Some asked questions about their own concerns or those pertaining to a loved one, and this was done on a one-to-one basis.

The way the afternoon was set up was very informal. What we basically did was place some information about dementia and local dementia services on each table, so you could just come in, have your tea, coffee or whatever you wanted.

If you wanted to ask a question confidentially on a one-to-one basis, Amy Murphy, our Southern Dementia Advisor based in Mallow, was available to answer such questions, and, of course, Helena and I were also there to help in any way.

Leaflets with practical information about living and coping at home, either for a person with dementia or their carer, were available and all conversations were held in total confidence.

Because it was such a large success, we have continued this format and Amy Murphy is always in attendance. And, due to their significant contribution to this success, I would like to acknowledge and thank Patricia Moylan, proprietor of the Daily Grind, and her wonderful staff for providing the facility to enable us to host our dementia café.

One thing that has been highlighted to me was the misconception that I had about The Alzheimer Society of Ireland being only for people with the Alzheimer type of dementia. That is simply not the case. As a person living with the Lewy body type of dementia and their carer, both Helena and I have received great assistance from them over the years.

Before I was asked to become a member of the Society's working group, I also had the misconception that this group, for want of a better word, was just for the older person with dementia. But, as it was pointed out to me, it is for all ages, and everyone is welcome. There are a lot of younger people with dementia and their carers who attend.

As I have said on many occasions, I am so lucky to have a wonderful GP and medical team and that is very important to me because I always get answers to any questions I may have.

What has come to light for me on several occasions, is that some people who are worried about themselves or a loved one, are not getting the proper answers to some of the questions that they raise with their doctors. They also are not being made aware of the services that are available to those who have dementia.

When you or a loved one go to your doctor, please make sure that you are heard and understood, and that if the doctor is not sure or not able to give you the answers to your questions, then you need to ask or maybe even insist that you are sent for further investigation. It's your health and your peace of mind that is at stake here, so don't be afraid to ask the pertinent questions. You may not always like the answer but believe me when I say that the relief of knowing one way or the other, brings a type of resolution to your worries.

Remember that people can and do live well with dementia, and the diagnosis not only affects the person who has it, but their families as well. With an average of over 6,000 people with dementia in County Cork alone, we must acknowledge that it affects our whole community.

Sometime after we had started up the Dementia Café in Kanturk, both Helena and I became involved in a new national organization called The Irish Dementia Café Network, which had been launched in September 2020. We were part of the setup of the organization which included developing what the key features of a dementia café should be, along with establishing the pillars and principles as well as the guidelines for running a dementia café. The end result is that every dementia café in Ireland is now registered with the organization and it's very easy to find a location on their website.

When I started to write this piece, we were meeting in the Daily Grind Café face-to-face, but since then, the COVID-19 pandemic has hit us and put an end to the dementia café in the coffee shop. But, like everything else with the pandemic, it took some getting used to and we then started to look for a way to move forward in spite of it.

We have had to adapt due to COVID-19, so with the help of some wonderful people, we now host our Kanturk Dementia Café virtually through Zoom™. They have been very successful for us, so much so, that whenever the pandemic is over and restrictions are lifted, we intend to use both the face-to-face meetings and incorporate the Zoom™ meetings as well.

The format to the meeting is quite simple. We have a guest speaker each month who speaks on a particular topic which could be dementia but could also be on general health and wellbeing.

But we also like to have some fun…

Our Zoom™ meeting in December was one of fun and festive celebration with lots of gratitude for coming through the tough year gone by in lock down. We also enjoyed both songs and storytelling from the wonderful Listowel entertainer, Frances Kennedy.

The important part of our dementia café is that there is always time for questions and answers, not only about the day's topic, but personal concerns that someone may bring up. The café is a safe place to ask a question and that is why it is so important for us to have our Dementia Advisor present.

The COVID-19 pandemic has brought very little good, but the one positive thing to come out of it for us, is the facility to have Zoom™ meetings. Video conferencing enables people who otherwise would not have the means to go to a café to join us.

## Chapter 9

## EMOTIONS AROUND DEMENTIA AND PRACTICAL ARRANGEMENTS FOR THE FUTURE

There's emotion around everything in life, whether good or bad, and each one of us are full of it. People show emotion in different ways. Some are good to hold it in and hide their emotions, I however am not. I could best be described at times as a 'Blubbering Mess'.

Different people deal with their emotions in unique ways, and I can tell you that no matter what way you deal with yours, it's your way of dealing with them and that's ok. I believe that it's healthy to get your emotions out and just as good as it is to have a good laugh, it's also ok to have a good cry every now and then. And, if you want to go and have a cry alone that's ok too.

Hearing the words 'Alzheimer's dementia', or any other type of dementia, can leave us feeling shocked, no matter how much we may have expected the diagnosis. The same can be said for any disease, thinking that there is something wrong and finding out for definite brings out two entirely different emotions. You face the task of trying to understand what dementia means and of adjusting to the life-changing impact of this condition. The range of emotions you, your loved one or your family may feel include:

### Disbelief and denial

These emotions are very common and are often a way of coping, as they provide time to understand and accept what the diagnosis means. However, they can also be a source of frustration for other family members who do not experience disbelief or denial. It is very common for people within the same family to accept or understand a diagnosis at different times and in different ways.

### Relief

For me, this was a big one because we knew that there was something very wrong and, when I was finally diagnosed, there was relief that at least now we knew what it was. That's the way it is for a lot of families, the feeling of relief that, at last, a proper diagnosis has been made.

### Fear

This can be a totally natural reaction, especially if you have not expected to be diagnosed, or have been diagnosed with a type of dementia that maybe you have never heard of. It's only natural to be fearful and it can very much be the fear of the unknown.

### Reluctance

Sometimes, it can be very hard on the carer to be thrust into a position of caregiving. Being reluctant to become a carer or part of a support team can become a real battle for some people.

### Guilt

Guilt can occur even though developing dementia is not anyone's fault. People can feel guilty for not being understanding or patient or for being angry and frustrated. Guilty that you don't want to be a carer and it's ok to feel that way. Some people have a hard time with it, but you cannot help the way you feel.

### Loss and sadness

These emotions can be felt by the entire family, as well as by the person who has been diagnosed with dementia. Loss and sadness about the things a person may not be able to do in the future, for the changes that may occur in a relationship, and in future plans. Sadness at watching someone no longer being able to work or do the things in life that they once loved. For example, sadness that a person can no longer drive, that alone takes away a person's independence and that can be devastating to watch.

### Frustration and anger

These can erupt when dementia enters your world and changes your life. You feel helpless to stop it, and, again, these can be just plain and simple natural reactions.

### Loneliness and isolation

These emotions can be quite overwhelming, as many people feel they are alone once a diagnosis is made. Even when surrounded by people, you can feel lonely in a crowded room. It is normal to feel different things at different times and it can be hard to deal with these emotions.

My advice would be if you are being overwhelmed by any of these emotions, don't bottle them up, talk to someone, either a professional or maybe just a friend. There is help out there and you don't have to be alone on your journey.

Other little things that might help...

Consider keeping a journal or diary. Write down how you are feeling day to day or week to week. This can help you understand what you are feeling and why. It can also help if you feel overwhelmed as it helps you organize your thoughts.

Talking to others about how you are feeling can really be a benefit. Think about joining a support group and meeting other people who also have a loved one who has been diagnosed with dementia can be a very positive experience. Support groups can provide a safe place to talk, to learn more about dementia and about ways to get help and support. There are also a number of online forums and groups where you can connect with others in similar situations.

When any illness enters our lives, it can be difficult to think about practical arrangements for the future. However, it is important to consider and seek advice about legal and financial affairs as early as possible.

A diagnosis of dementia does not automatically mean that a person cannot make financial and legal decisions. While a person has the capacity to outline their wishes and to understand the effects of a legal or financial decision then they can continue to make such decisions. A person with dementia in the early stages of the condition may still be able to make plans in this area. A person in middle or later stages of the condition may not be able to do this. If you and your loved one are not sure about whether these decisions can be made, check with your doctor or solicitor. If possible, your loved one with dementia should be involved in the process.

Visit a solicitor to make a will if they have not already done so. They should also choose a person to manage legal, financial and certain personal care decisions if they are not able to do this for themselves in the future. This involves setting up an Enduring Power of Attorney [EPA], which must

# Chapter 10

# HALLUCINATIONS AND DELUSIONS

I will try to help you understand the changes in behaviour that can and do occur with people such as myself who suffer from this ugly disease called dementia. As I have explained in earlier articles, dementia is an umbrella term for all types of dementia and there are over 400 different types of dementia *(understandtogether.ie)*. No two people are affected in the same way, they may have similar symptoms, but as each person is unique, so is the way that dementia affects them. As I have already used this saying, 'When you have met one person with dementia, you have met one person with dementia'. That explains that no two people are the same.

This week I want to talk about *Hallucinations and Delusions* as they form a big part of the type of dementia that I have been diagnosed with, namely Lewy Body Dementia. These symptoms are not confined solely to Lewy Body Dementia as people with other types of dementia may also experience hallucinations. They may hear, see, smell, taste or feel things that are not really there. Hallucinations involving sight or hearing are the most common (that is definitely true in my case), although I have smelled things that are not real as well.

The reaction of a person with dementia to the hallucination may vary:

1. They may realise that their imagination is playing tricks with them and pay no attention to the hallucination.

2. They might find it difficult to decide whether or not the hallucination is real. In such instances, they might find it reassuring if you go with them to look at where they saw the imaginary object, or to check the room where they thought they heard voices or other noises. You can then confirm that there is nothing but be careful not to tell the person that they were imagining it, because to them it was real. Instead, try to reassure the person that everything is OK.

3. As the dementia becomes more severe, some people may become convinced that what they are seeing or hearing is real. This can be very frightening. For some, it is worth trying to let them know that although you cannot share their experience, you do understand that it is distressing for them. Try to distract them, again there is no point in arguing about whether or not what they are seeing is real, to the patient, I can tell you that it is very real.

For others who may have severe hallucinations, the carer should validate the person's experience, and let them know that they are safe. Check the environment and, if dark, turn on additional lights or move them to another room. Like above, you can try to distract them, but if that doesn't seem to work, then you might have to enter their hallucination world and in story-form attempt to convince them that you have taken care of the situation. Many carers become great storytellers.

4. Hallucinations may be less likely to occur when the person is occupied or interested in what is going on around them. (Although I have been busy and seen people who were not there.) If a person with dementia is distressed by their hallucinations or if the hallucinations persist, speak to your GP or neurologist as medication can sometimes help. I am on Donesyn (Donepezil) for the hallucinations and to improve cognition, and Rivotril® (Clonazepam) for the nightmares. Although these medications have helped me a little, the symptoms are not eliminated completely. It's also important for you to know that these and many other medications used to treat these symptoms can have serious side effects or can

sometimes have the complete opposite effect. If recommended by your doctor talk to them about starting at a low dose to minimize side effects.

Visual hallucinations are the most common type of hallucinations in dementia. The person may see people, animals or other objects. Sometimes the hallucinations involve quite complicated scenes or bizarre situations. Some people with dementia who experience visual hallucinations only experience them occasionally and they may only last for a few seconds but sometimes they are more persistent and troublesome. For me, so far, they only appear occasionally and for a few seconds but still can be very frightening.

Although visual hallucinations are a common symptom in LBD, there are other possible underlying causes which are treatable. Some can be the result of physical illness such as infections or the side effects of some types of medication. For me, one of the worst I experienced was while in the middle of a bad kidney infection.

Poor eyesight can also be a contributory factor, so it's important to get your eyes checked regularly and make sure that your glasses are always clean. In addition, always make sure that there is good lighting in a room as the darkness is not our friend. These are small things, I know, but can help a lot.

Another thing to check with your eye doctor or GP is if there are cataracts involved and should they be removed if the vision is being affected. Know that in the case of LBD, people usually experience hallucinations because of changes that are occurring in the brain as the disease progresses.

Auditory hallucinations occur when people hear voices or other noises although no one in their vicinity can hear those particular sounds. As with visual hallucinations, it is important to rule out possible causes such as physical illness and the side effects of medication. (Like myself, many LBD sufferers are hyper-sensitive to some medications.) It is also worth checking the person's hearing and make sure their hearing aid is working properly, if they wear one. Again, a small thing, but one that can make a massive difference.

One sign that a person may be having hallucinations involving hearing voices, is when they start talking to themselves and pause, as though waiting for someone else to finish what they are saying, before continuing. However, it is important to remember that not everyone who talks to themselves is having hallucinations. Shouting at people who are not there also suggests possible hallucinations.

Delusions are a different type of hallucination where people have a belief that they hold onto despite evidence to the contrary. People with dementia may become rather suspicious, accusing someone of stealing from them when something has been misplaced, for example. If they are in early stages, however, they are often reassured when the item is found. With some people this suspicion goes much farther, and they may develop distorted ideas about what is actually happening. They may be convinced that other people want to harm them for example, and no amount of evidence to the contrary will persuade them otherwise. Delusions can be very distressing, both for the person with dementia and the person close to them. According to The Alzheimer Society of Ireland some of the delusions that people with dementia have include the following:

1. Their partner is being unfaithful.

2. Their partner or close relative has been replaced by an imposter who closely resembles them.

3. Their home is not their own.

4. Their food is being poisoned.

5. Their neighbours are spying on them.

People with dementia have these odd ideas because of the changes that are occurring in their brain. There is often little point arguing with the person as this can cause further distress.

1. Try and reassure the person that you are on their side.

2. Distract them with other activities.

If you would like to have a chat with someone with regards to any of these, contact The Alzheimer Society of Ireland Helpline no: 1800 341 341 or sometimes it may be necessary to contact the public health nurse or the GP. If you live in another country look up organizations that address your specific dementia for information and resources. I talk about what I have written in more detail in my book, *Lewy Body Dementia, Survival and Me*.

*Kevin Quaid, 2019, The Vale Star*
*(Updated 2021)*

*I realise today that I have stopped living*

*I'm literally just trying to get to the next day*

*Just living in the thought of tomorrow*

*I'm not living, I'm waiting and the trouble is*

*I don't know exactly what I'm waiting for*

*I am a kind of scared of what it might be*

# Chapter 11

## DREAMS MADE OF NIGHTMARES

For a couple of months before going to see my neurologist, I would often wake in the mornings and tell Helena that my dreams were so real that it seemed like I was living in a completely different world. My dreams were so real and so detailed that it would take me a couple of minutes to figure out what was what upon wakening.

Now I use the word dreams lightly, as they were and still are nightmares, and the longer I have LBD, the worse they are getting. As each night passes, the amount and quality of sleep I am getting is less and less and some nights I might only get three hours. Let me give you a few examples of the nightmares I have.

One night I was dreaming that I was living in America in an apartment block, and while in a public toilet, I could see these two teenagers with what seemed like a quilt from a bed, and they were cutting it up in strips. I didn't want to say anything to them as I had a feeling that it was a bad area and as they had a knife, I didn't feel safe. I went outside and was talking to my uncle (who died from Alzheimer's in real life) and his daughters. When I went back in, one of the teenagers was hanging, having used the strips that they had cut from the quilt. I could see his eyes and the blood pouring from his mouth, so I ran for help, called the police and was not able to tell them the address. I was so in a panic that I gave the phone to a woman, told her to give them the address with instructions to tell them that we needed the ambulance, police and fire brigade.

Then I woke up and I was truly terrified. I took off my sleep apnoea mask and was so thirsty, but too terrified to get out of bed or even to look around. I called Helena and she got up with me, came as far as the bathroom with me, got me a drink then stayed up with me for about half an hour until the worst of the fear passed. That was at three o clock in the morning, and for the next two and a half hours, I lay in bed reliving the dream, terrified that someone would walk down the hall and into the bedroom. This is a very common thing at night, fear that someone will break in, that there is someone outside, or that we will be attacked.

Another dream I had was that I was driving along this beautiful country road on a motorbike which is something that I had never done. The place was very flat, and I could see all around me and-could actually feel the breeze in my face, but in the dream, I had no idea whether the experience was real or if I was dreaming. So, as I was approaching this village, I saw a big gable end of a house in front of me and the road turning a sharp right, then thought to myself, 'What if I speed up and just drive the bike at full speed into the wall and try to kill myself (since I'm not wearing a helmet), then I will either die or wake up?' But then the thought hit me, 'If I kill myself, maybe I will die in my sleep.' Again, I woke up terrified and, as always, couldn't go back to sleep.

I will give you one more example of a nightmare, one that is pretty disturbing and kept repeating for several nights. Even thinking about it now frightens me.

For some reason, I was involved in murdering a man and had the body buried in a ditch. The murder had taken place a good few months back, and every night I could feel the worry creeping up on me. 'What if the body is ever discovered, I could wind up in jail? What will my friends think of me, especially as one of my friends is a policeman?'

I have no idea who was murdered or why, but it was again terrifying to be living in this nightmare and living with all the worry and stress of it. So, I decided to move the body to where, I do not know. All I remember was looking at this rotting corpse of a man and the horrible smell, then suddenly I woke out of the nightmare. But all that day, the one thing that didn't leave me was the smell. It was so bad that Helena had to go to the health shop for orange essential oil for me to put some under my nostrils to try to get rid of it.

This is after being up and awake for at least six hours at this stage. The frightening thing about the nightmares is waking up from them, and not being able to go back to sleep. In most cases, I'm afraid to go back to sleep just in case I end up back in the same dream, which often happens. There are days when all that I can think about are the nightmares from the night before and I can get so caught up in them that before I know it, my day has gone, and the cycle starts all over again.

I can honestly say at this stage that the worst part of the LBD for me is the nights. On at least two occasions, I have woken up from another terrifying nightmare, looked at my wife, Helena, asleep alongside me, and shouted at her, 'WHO ARE YOU?' It is only when she has spoken, that I realise who she is and, again, she has the job of comforting me, telling me that everything is ok, and that I am at home in my own bed.

I suppose every disease affects those who are closest to you, but I can say, none more so than LBD, because my wife has as many sleepless nights as I do. When she does sleep, I don't think she gets a proper sleep because she is so conscious of what I am going through and at times is probably worried am I going to attack her by acting out one of my dreams.

I could write books about the different dreams, but there is no point. None of them are about lying on a beach somewhere sipping a cocktail, instead, they are all about murder, death and mayhem.

My worst nightmare is if I were to do anything to hurt my wife, and it is something that we have had to discuss. If the day comes that she thinks that she is in any danger, then we will have to consider different rooms or else a dementia home of some sort. It is so important to discuss all these issues with your loved ones especially when your mind is still pretty good.

*You're never too old to learn new things*

# Chapter 12

# TECHNOLOGY AND HOW IT CAN HELP

This is another article that I found people really liked and I wasn't aware that a lot of the things mentioned in the article aren't available in many locations. As I said in the last chapter, some parts of Ireland are very rural and a lot of people live on their own, but there is a true saying that 'you can be alone in a crowd', so for that reason, I wrote this article. It's for people everywhere, whether you are in a big city or in the heart of the country.

We live in a world that is full of technology and it's probably fair to say that it's impossible to keep up with it. It seems to me that kids are quicker than adults to pick things up, especially technology. My two beautiful granddaughters, Hollie age 11 and Victoria age 5, would put me to shame. I suppose the question is, 'How can assistive technology help?' Well, it can help in the following ways.

- *Help you to live more independently*
- *Provide support and reassurance*
- *Reduce risk of accidents*

Assistive technology can help you do things like:

- *Remember days, dates and time*
- *Find things*
- *Take your medication on time*

- *Keep in touch with family and friends*
- *Continue to do things that you have always done*
- *Let you know if the gas or electric is left on*
- *Let you know if a tap is left running*
- *Raise an alarm*
- *Let people know where you are if you become lost or disorientated*

Now it's important to remember that we are all unique and that assistive technology will not suit everyone. You may have to try different options to find solutions that suit you. Assistive technology has lots of benefits, but like everything in life, it also has its limitations. My recommendations are just a sample of products and technology that are available and new technology is coming on stream all the time, e.g., tracking devices that integrate with mobile phones and assistive apps are constantly being developed to make life easier for the person with the disease.

Remember that technology can never replace human contact nor eliminate risk, and like everything, some can be expensive. Here is a list of some items and their benefits.

### Clocks with Calendars

1. The Clairmont PLC Large Day/Night Flip Calendar Clock is an analogue clock, which uses

the traditional clock hands to show the time, automatically changes every day, and clearly shows the day, the date, the time, and whether its day or night.

2. The DayClox®, a digital format clock, displays the day, the date, the time, and again, whether it's day or night.

3. Then you have what's called the MemRabel® dementia clock which is a calendar clock similar to the DayClox®, however, it has more features. For example, it can play pre-recorded messages at times set by you or your family. These messages might be a reminder to take medication, or to take the bins out. It can play up to 20 messages a day. They have several models each designed with a variety of features depending on your needs.

### Prompts and Reminders

*To do notes.* Use sticky–backed notes to help remind you of things like, what you have to do or how to do something. Be sure to put the notes near to where you need them, for example, near an appliance or on a remote control.

*Pictures and signs.* A simple picture can be useful to prompt you to remember where and what certain items are. For example, you might put a picture of socks on your sock drawer. A sign beside the cooker (stove) can be a reminder to switch off the mains when you've finished cooking.

**Checklist.** A checklist can be another simple way to prompt you to complete a task. One example would be a list of things that you need to do before going to bed, such as: lock the door, turn off the television, empty ashtrays, put up the fireguard, and take your medication, and so on.

### Item Finder

There is a device called Loc8Tor™, which will direct you to your keys, phone or wallet, and it can find things up to 400 feet away.

### Voice Prompter

A timed wander reminder *(alzproducts.co.uk)* is a motion sensor that can play a pre-recorded message when you pass it by. This can be useful for when you leave the house, and you worry you will forget your keys. The message can simply play 'Remember your keys'. Some also come with a timer so it can play a pre-recorded message at certain times during the day or night which would be very helpful if your loved one with dementia is a wanderer and needs a gentle reminder to return to bed.

### Automatic Pill Dispenser

The Pivotell® automatic pill dispenser is helpful for reminding you when to take your medication. It is turned on at certain times each day, like a lamp in the evening.

## Bath Plug

The Magiplug® is a special bathplug. As your bath fills, the Magiplug® recognises when there is enough water in the bath. If the water goes over this level, the Magiplug® releases the plug and allows the water to flow out preventing flooding. It is very useful if you find yourself running a bath and you become distracted (like the phone rings) and you forget that the tap is running.

## Bath Alarm

The Brother Max® alarm is useful if you sometimes forget to test the temperature of the water in the bath. It will sound an alarm if the temperature is below or above the range set by you and your family.

## Motion Sensor Night Light

If, like me, you wake at night and get out of bed, the Lifemax® motion-sensor night light will sense your movement and a light will come on allowing you to walk safely. The light will stay lit for one minute unless it detects more movement. You can put these sensors anywhere in your home.

Technology is changing all the time and what is important to remember, if it works for you then that's okay. We all don't have to keep up to date with the latest advancements in technology unless it comes recommended to us and we are comfortable using it.

*Kevin Quaid, 2019, The Vale Star*
*(Updated 2021)*

Between them they have won every accolade that the game of hurling has to offer and have played at the highest level.

To say that I am proud of them is an understatement, twinged with a small bit of jealousy, that I was never as good as they were on the GAA (Gaelic Athletic Association) pitch even though I often dreamed of playing for Limerick or at least being part of that illustrious group. This never happened while I was in good health, during my working life or indeed while playing sports, but it did happen in 2019, two years after I was diagnosed with Lewy Body Dementia, when I was able to put aside my walking frame and able to walk with just the aid of a walking stick.

Helena and I were having a coffee in Mallow, County Cork, with a good friend of ours, Kathy Ryan. Kathy was chair of the Irish Dementia Working Group (IDWG) at the time, and we started to talk about how our diseases were progressing. We were both diagnosed with young-onset dementia, and Kathy has Alzheimer's dementia. We started to talk about The Alzheimer Society of Ireland and about fundraising. We were discussing how we could help when I got the idea that we should have a game of hurling between County Limerick and County Tipperary. (I'm from Limerick and Kathy from Tipperary.) I thought it was a brilliant idea, but at this stage, it was only an idea, and I knew that I had to only make one phone call for it to become a reality.

That call was to my cousin, who I spoke about earlier, the one we affectionately call 'Joe the Goalie'. I explained what we had in mind and asked whether he could get a team together. His reply was, 'Absolutely! No problem. I will contact the boys and we will get the team together.'

Another man that I have to thank here is Michael Cleary from Nenagh in County Tipperary for his organization of the Tipperary team. Like the Quaid's, Michael has won every honour that can be won on the hurling field, and he was actually a customer of mine when I was a salesman in the early 1980s.

The next thing that we had to do was tell The Alzheimer Society of Ireland of our plans and they put me in touch with a wonderful lady, Máiréad Dillion. She is their head of fundraising and was brilliant leaving no stone unturned to make this game happen and made sure all the stops were pulled out. It was billed as **The Legends Hurling Clash between Limerick and Tipperary** to be played for the **Kevin Quaid and Kathy Ryan Legends Cup**.

The game took place on Saturday, 7th September 2019 at 5 pm. It was played in Nenagh in County Tipperary and the goodwill and help of the people from the club in Nenagh who gave their grounds and encouragement were scarce, but the laughter we had for those couple of minutes is something that will live with me forever.

I went into the Tipperary dressing room and thanked them for their efforts and again the reception that I got was awesome for a Limerick man in a Tipp dressing room. Again, I couldn't hold back the tears.

Time for the game. As the band started playing both teams lined up behind them. Kathy Ryan led out the Tipperary team and Kevin Quaid led out the Limerick team. As we walked onto the field with the pipe band, I could hear the cheers over the loud music. I just thought to myself, even though I have this disease, which is both progressive and incurable, this would not have even been remotely possible but for the fact that I have it. For a brief moment in time, I didn't mind having this disease. Both teams lined up in front of the stand and each and every player were introduced to the crowd along with Kathy and me.

Tipperary won the match and both Kathy and I presented the cup to Michael Cleary, the Tipperary Captain. After the game, a lot of the crowd mixed with the players on the field. For that day, the Limerick team consisted of not one, but five Quaid's; Joe Quaid, John Quaid, Gerry Quaid, and me, Kevin Quaid. In addition, our two beautiful mascots just happened to be Gerry's granddaughter, Laurin Markham, and my own beautiful granddaughter, Hollie Ballantine Quaid.

As the crowd was mingling on the field, one of the men who was a particular hero of mine came over to me in tears and put his two hands around me and thanked me so much for the day. He said that he was thinking especially of his Mom and Dad who had both unfortunately passed away from Lewy Body Dementia. He said that I would never know what it meant to him to hear people talk openly about this type of dementia. We spoke about the stigma and how we hoped that the day would come when there was no more stigma around any form of dementia.

After the game, the current Limerick manager, John Kiely, presented me with a signed hurley. It had been signed by both teams and he made a very moving speech about what both Kathy and me, and all we had done. After, we went on to the hotel where we enjoyed good food, drinks and music. I have wonderful memories of the speeches that were made that night and the wonderful things that were said.

So, you see it is said, 'the darkest hour is just before the dawn' and I believed one of my darkest days was the day I was given the diagnosis of Lewy Body Dementia. But since my diagnosis, I have never given up on my dreams and I have had what I can only describe as 'WOW moments'. This hurling match was full of many WOW moments for me... the day that Kevin Quaid managed and lead out the famous Limerick hurling team to play Tipperary.

# Chapter 14

**A photo captures a moment in time while giving a lifetime of memories**

Beautiful portrait of Robin Williams
By artist Kunle Adelwale

**Kevin during one of his many radio interviews**

**Podcasts available On YouTube**

**Kevin and his granddaughter Hollie at the launch of Feathers in my Brain, a book to explain dementia to younger children**

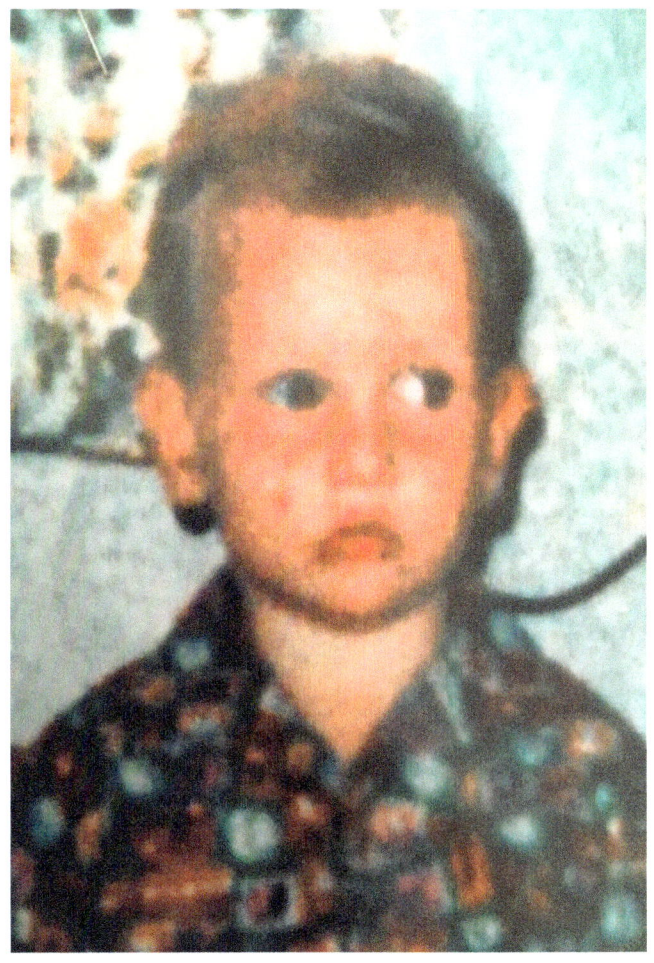

Kevin as a little boy did not know what the future would hold for him and how Lewy body dementia would consume his brain and life

# Chapter 15

## THIS CHRISTMAS

### *'Remember those who can't remember'*

This chapter is a combination of a couple of articles that I wrote at the end of 2019 and early 2020, one for Christmas and the other for the New Year.

### *Christmas*

The following two sayings you will no doubt have seen from time to time. The first one, 'Understand Together', can be seen in Irish TV ads presented with real people who have been diagnosed with different forms of dementia. The other saying, 'Remember Those Who Can't Remember', is probably better known around the world as a slogan for those who live with dementia. I thought it would be a fitting way to talk about having Christmas with your loved one who has dementia, whether it be someone with young-onset, early stage, middle stage, late stage, or for those who have already passed.

Most of us think of Christmas as a fun-filled, happy time of year, especially in a home with children anticipating a visit from Santa Claus who's bringing all those wonderful gifts, or even in houses where there are family and relatives coming to stay for the holidays.

We have all seen the films with the snow and the happy endings and that's true in lots of cases in homes all over the world. But there is another side to Christmas which, for some, can be extremely lonely and very sad. This time of year can be very isolating for a lot of people, and not just for those who live with dementia, but for those who live alone or others who may not have many callers throughout this festive season. So please just keep them in mind this holiday season and maybe pop in to visit and wish them a Happy Christmas.

I also want to talk a little about people who are living with dementia and how to enjoy Christmas with them.

From my perspective, if your loved one with dementia is still at home and there is family around, try to make this Christmas one of the best they have ever had; go all out, buy the extra-large turkey, enjoy the company of friends and family, and allow them to eat and drink to their heart's content. But it's important that you remember that your loved one may tire or become confused or anxious with all the noise, so I suggest that you have a plan for them to take a break or even a rest in a quiet, separate room so they can continue on later and enjoy the day.

Now, I am speaking to the person in the early stages of dementia or who may have been just diagnosed this year. Even though you may have had a miserable year and have gotten a diagnosis of dementia, don't let it beat you. Instead, say, 'to hell with this dementia', we are going to have the Christmas of a lifetime and one that we will never forget, or, at the very least, try and make it as normal as possible and don't let a diagnosis ruin what can be one of the happiest times of the year. One that you and your family can look back on in years to come and be able to laugh and cry about.

This year, I know that's what I'm going to do, as I will be spending it with some of my family that I didn't get to see last year. We are going to have a ball and Lewy Body Dementia is not going to stop me from having a wonderful Christmas. I certainly will not let Lewy ruin Christmas for my wife, Helena, and my wonderful family.

Now let's talk about the people with dementia who are in respite or care home facilities who are allowed home for Christmas.

Being able to go home for the holiday is truly a blessing, and hopefully, a happy time, even though I know it might be tinged with a hint of sadness, but the fact that your loved one is home for Christmas, please embrace it. Be happy that you can spend this time with them and please include them in as much of the activities as possible, whether it is helping with the shopping, cooking or getting ready around the house. Try to look past the disease and see the person and remember what they used to love. Then try to bring some of those beloved memories and traditions into the Christmas that you are having at your home.

Then there is the person who is in the late stages of dementia and may not be able to come home for any part of Christmas. Please make the time to visit that person, sit and talk to them about

Christmas, and reminisce about Christmas' gone by and the good times you enjoyed together. Just because they may not be able to respond to you, I have found that it is very likely they can hear you, and, again, it might bring back happy childhood memories and just might make Christmas more joyful for them as well as yourself.

Finally, we'll look at those who have lost a loved one over the last twelve months and how they might enjoy the holiday without that person with them.

The truth is, yes, loss of a loved one is very hard, but if you gather with other family members, talk to each other about them, share stories of the good times, and although there may be tears, I bet you some wonderful memories will come to the surface. In a lot of cases, this reminiscence of your missing loved one will lead to laughter, especially when recalling a funny incident or a happier time. In the end, I can assure you that you and your family will start to feel a little better and maybe even a little closer, but one thing's for sure, you will feel the love of the person who has gone to Heaven.

'Remember Those Who Can't Remember' and try and be there for them. I wish you nothing but the best this Christmas and please have a Happy and Holy Christmas, stay strong and look after one another.

*Kevin Quaid, 2019, The Vale Star (Updated 2021)*

This is part of the second article that I wrote at the end of 2019 and the beginning of 2020.

### A New Year - A New Start

I would like to wish each and every one of you a happy New Year and may this year be one of the best you've ever had.

Always, at the end of the year, it's time to reflect on what type of year it's been and, no doubt, for a lot of people it will be a year to remember. Yet, for others, it will be a year to forget.

My year started off on a high. While visiting my family in Australia, I met with a wonderful lady named Sally Lambourne, who is General Manager of Consumer Engagement for Dementia Australia, and it was great to see the similarities and the differences in the way in which Ireland and Australia treat people who live with dementia.

At the current time, Australia has dementia centres in Darwin, Brisbane, Sydney, Melbourne, Canberra, Perth, and the final one in Hobart in Tasmania. I am delighted to tell you that in each of their centres, they have a library and among their books is my first book, **Lewy Body Dementia, Survival and Me.**

(Personally, completing a book has been an amazing achievement for me and it's being reinforced, most weeks, when I get emails from people all over the world thanking me for writing it.)

According to the World Health Organization (WHO), there is a person diagnosed with dementia every three seconds and it is becoming an epidemic. Unlike Ireland, Dementia Australia gets funding from both state and federal governments, whereas, The Alzheimer Society of Ireland (ASI) has to put in a pre-budget submission every year and only hope that they will receive funding. Most of the time they get little or no funding, which is sad considering the number of people with dementia.

Despite such lack of funding, The Alzheimer Society of Ireland, along with its wonderful staff and CEO Pat Mc

Loughlin, continue to do amazing work for the thousands who currently live with dementia and for the 30 additional individuals a day who are being diagnosed. Even being underfunded, it is clear to me that Ireland is up there with the leading countries in the care that we provide and for that, I am truly grateful, because without the ASI my life would be in a completely different place.

I often wonder what is it about people and why is there still stigma and shame surrounding dementia? It's not just an Irish thing, I have found that it's just as bad in Australia and, most likely, many other countries, as well. When will people get it into their heads that the person with dementia is not letting on that they have it, their doctors are not making it up and their scans may not always reveal the whole story? Because the word dementia is what we call an 'umbrella' term, the diagnosis people receive may be one of dementia, however, the type of dementia can be one of many and, please understand, that not all dementia sufferers have memory problems.

Lewy Body Dementia is what I like to call, night-time dementia, because in my case, I have found that I can have some brilliant days. Some days may seem to me and others, very normal and a good day, but my nights, can go from bad to horrific in no time at all, with increased confusion and terrifying nightmares.

I also find the wintertime very difficult, and the darkness is not my friend, but I was lucky to spend the last couple of months with our children in Australia (December 2019 - February 2020) and without them, the trip would not have been possible. Being in a warmer climate for 3 months, has made the winter very short and, as we approach the spring, there is, as we say, 'a great stretch in the evenings'.

I find that the heat is very good for my pains and while I do realise that not everyone can go to where it is warm, if you suffer from pain because of the type of dementia that you have, why not try and go to a heated swimming pool for exercise. You may also find that they have saunas and steam rooms that might be beneficial for you for short periods of time. Beware though, high temperatures may cause you to experience serious symptoms, so speak with your doctor before using a sauna or steam room and follow his/her recommendations.

Another thing that I do for pain management is take CBD oil and have found it very beneficial as well. I just put a few drops under my tongue in the mornings before I have my tea or coffee. Again, check with your doctor before adding CBD to your regimen as there are varying combinations and dosages and in many locations around the world it has not been legalized for medical use.

At year end, I don't want us to forget about the families who have lost loved ones whether it be to dementia or any other illness or injury. Indeed, that has been true of our family as well, as we lost my beloved cousin, Theresa Quaid, through cancer. It was with her help and encouragement that I had the courage to write my first book, **Lewy Body Dementia, Survival and Me**, and it was because of that encouragement that I dedicated it to her. We also lost another beautiful lady with, coincidentally, the very same name, Theresa Quaid, and through cancer as well; both taken at a young age and way too soon. For me, the year was mixed with every kind of emotion, from wonderful highs to depressing lows, but here I am again, out the other side of it, and I do think a lot stronger and better for it.

Guess what I have found out (and I am being sarcastic)? DEMENTIA IS NOT CONTAGIOUS! So, please talk normally to those you know who live with dementia and don't treat us as if we have a disease that you might catch. Each and every one of us can help those with dementia and the person at home caring for them. Know that the carers are often in more need of support than the person who has dementia, because they are the people who live and watch it progress twenty-four hours a day, seven days a week.

So, as this is my New Year's message, I intend to completely focus on the positive and will try each and every day not to let this horrible disease take over my life. Instead, I intend to live as normal and as full a life as possible. I hope this year brings you all the goodness that you deserve.

*Kevin Quaid, 2019, The Vale Star*
*(Updated 2021)*

## Chapter 16

## 30 PEOPLE PER DAY IN IRELAND AND 1 EVERY 3 SECONDS IN THE REST OF THE WORLD ARE GIVEN A DEMENTIA DIAGNOSIS

What frightening statistics... 'In Ireland 30 people are diagnosed with dementia each day,[11] and worldwide, it is estimated that a person is diagnosed with dementia every 3 seconds[12].'

*It's going to be an epidemic, or maybe it is one already.*

I have been told that years ago, when TB (tuberculosis) was a major problem in this country, it carried a stigma with it. When cancer started to become the problem, there again, a stigma got attached to it, and now we arrive at dementia, and it happens to be the latest disease being stigmatized.

There is probably not a family that hasn't been touched by cancer, but thankfully the stigma that was attached to it is now long gone. As dementia of all types are now being spoken about more and

---

[11] *Alzheimer Europe (2020), Dementia in Europe Yearbook 2019* **Estimating the prevalence of dementia in Europe**
[12] *World Health Organisation (WHO), 2020,* **Global status report on the public health response to dementia**

more, my hope is that the stigma around it might someday be gone also.

Recently, during a very busy week (a period that I enjoyed no end), I met some fantastic people. I was given the opportunity to speak to a large company gathering of around 120 employees in Shannon.

The company (GECAS) has taken it upon itself to highlight different problems that families have and formed a group called The GECAS Diversity and Inclusiveness Council. The aim of the group is to raise awareness and to highlight issues that people in Ireland face on a daily basis. That week the topic was *Dementia*, and both Helena and I were invited to address the issues that surround us daily as we live with Lewy Body Dementia; the disease that I have been diagnosed with and Helena lives with as my spousal carer. They wanted to educate their staff about this challenging disease.

A couple of things became very clear, very quickly. The first thing I noticed was how young the staff were and was surprised by how many had been affected by or, at the very least, knew someone with some form of dementia. The love, support and compassion shown to both Helena, and I was unreal. The fact that so many of their staff took time out of their busy schedules to sit and listen to us talk about our experience with one type of dementia was indeed very humbling. It makes me feel so good that younger people show such an interest and want to do something about raising awareness around dementia. This fills me with hope as they are our future, and some may even have a role to play as a future carer to a loved one with dementia.

To see companies like this, take such a leading role in highlighting the plight of families with dementia has to be a brilliant thing and will, of course, make a difference.

One evening, we were invited to University College Cork (UCC) to give a talk to a large group who attended at the request of Professor Nicole Müller, the head of Speech and Hearing Sciences in the School of Clinical Therapies. Again, the amount of young people present who evidently had a relative suffering from any one of the various forms of dementia was amazing.

After our presentation, we had a question-and-answer session and this, once again, highlighted the fact that we as a society have such a lot to learn about these diseases and how to cope and live well with dementia.

It is possible to live a fairly normal and pretty good life once we know what the warning signs are, what the pitfalls are, what to watch for, and then educate ourselves on how to manage the symptoms and live our daily life in the best way possible. I suppose the most important thing that we can do for someone living with dementia is:

- When talking to a patient with dementia, if they say something that doesn't make sense, instead of correcting them, try and go into their world to find out how they see things, what they are feeling, and what they believe is real.

- If they make a request that you don't agree with, what's the harm in going along, as long as it is safe and reasonable to do so?

That brings me to St. Columcille's Hospital in Loughlinstown, County Dublin, for the opening of the Memory Technology Resource Room and Gardens. There, we were met by Anna de Suin from the National Dementia Office.

It's a beautiful facility and one of many that are being opened all over the country. Their aim is to show people what is available to assist the person with dementia in their daily life and how using these aids will hopefully help to make their carer's life a little easier and maybe a little less stressful.

People can go and spend time there enjoying the beautiful garden and, at the same time, get practical help for living an independent life at home with their families. These facilities can be, and should be, recommended by your local GP. If not, you can go to them yourself and find out about their offerings.

The technology that is available nowadays is unbelievable, from adapted phones with a person's face on it (if you need to call your loved one, you don't even have to look up their phone number), to clocks that show the time, date, year, and day in big print, etc. It is the small things like these that can make a big difference in people's lives.

We are very lucky to have a wonderful place in Mallow in the Primary Health Care Centre called the Memory Room. It's looked after by Amy Murphy our wonderful Southern Dementia Advisor (you'll remember Amy from the Dementia Café).

The Memory Room is well worth a visit, and you would be amazed at the number of simple things that are available to make the life of the person with dementia and their carer a lot easier. If you would like to visit the Memory Room in Mallow you should ask your GP about the service and indeed all the other services that are available for families who are dealing with dementia of all types.

It may certainly be a long road, but together, we can help one another to make the best out of every day. So please take the opportunity to reach out to help those who might be finding this disease a little hard to deal with, and remember... 'it is in giving, we receive' *(St Francis of Assisi)*.

# Chapter 17

# SETTING LIMITS AND FROM SEEING RED TO GOING RED

It's been another busy period in my life, and you didn't hear from me last week because we had a family wedding. For me, and I know from speaking to a lot of people who have dementia, weddings can sometimes be a frightening experience. Frightening might be the wrong word; maybe I ought to call it overwhelming or a combination of both. But we planned this one around my challenges and it made it so much easier and a lot more enjoyable.

Consider what a long day it can be for the likes of me with dementia. From the time you leave home to get to the church for the marriage ceremony with all its formalities, and then by the time the wedding feast is finished, nine or ten hours may have passed. This time I checked into the hotel where the wedding was on and spent the day resting and watching a bit of television. By the time the wedding party arrived for the rest of their celebrations, I was well refreshed and able to enjoy the gorgeous meal and I had a wonderful sociable enjoyable evening. The fact that everyone knows that I have Lewy Body Dementia meant that everyone understood that I wouldn't be able for the long day and all the family were delighted that I was there for the meal and able to enjoy the evening. I know my limits and I know what I am able for and even though sometimes I need to push myself a little, that's OK. I always need to remember to not push myself too far because, if I do, I suffer the consequences of confusion and total exhaustion.

Anyway, back to my headline 'FROM SEEING RED TO GOING RED'.

What I mean by that is on Wednesday 13th March, I was asked to be one of the speakers at the all-party committee that deal with dementia in the AV room in Leinster House. There were over 70 politicians in attendance and here are approximate figures from that day.

A big thank you to Michael Moynihan TD (Teachta Dála or Member of Parliament) and the FF party for their attendance, as between Senators and TDs, accounted for approximately 50. We also had TDs from every single party including Independents, Labour and most of the smaller parties, but only two secretaries from the actual Government. No one from the Department of Health, not even a representative... this was one of the reasons that I saw red.

I addressed them about the lack of dementia advisors in the whole of Ireland as we have only 9 dementia advisors like Amy Murphy who works out of the Memory Room in Mallow. We need a minimum of 90, but if we could get 19 for the moment, it would be a start. I tried to impress upon them how serious the problem of dementia is and that it's only going to get worse with approximately 30 people a day being diagnosed with some form of dementia. These politicians are the people in power, and they are the people who can and should make the change. The CEO of The Alzheimer Society, who was also in the audience, also pleaded for help and I was glad to see that what we said was taken on board. Within a matter of 15 minutes, Michael Moynihan TD spoke about it on the floor of the Dáil Éireann and reminded the government that it is part of the supply and confidence agreement. So, let's wait and see what happens and if there is an update, I will let you know. So that is why I saw RED.

Again, on the theme going red, which doesn't mean that I was embarrassed or put my foot in it. (By the way if I did, it wouldn't be my first time.)

Helena and I were asked to go on the Neil Prendeville Show on Cork's RedFM 104-106, last Tuesday March 19th. Can I start by saying what a lovely gentleman he really is and was so genuinely interested in my condition? Once again, the response to the show was unbelievable and shows the hunger out there for information about dementia. Not only was it broadcast live on the radio, it also went out live in their Facebook™ page. (At the time of writing this article it has over 11,000 hits.)

That night, I got emails and messages from Australia, the Caribbean, the Netherlands, and Lanzarote, not to mention all the emails from Ireland and the UK. (At the same time, I must not forget to thank the people from the Republic of Cork for their wonderful and continued support and love.) All this outpouring of interest evidences the need for openness and honesty about dementia and the need to get rid of the horrible stigma that surrounds it.

I keep going on about the stigma and shame that some people still associate with the word dementia and unfortunately it is still out there. But we won't carry that stigma any longer with us, as we see the love and support expressed by the people who know me and by many who are complete strangers. For that I am truly grateful.

*Kevin Quaid, 2019, The Vale Star*
*(Updated 2021)*

*Keep banging on the door of life
and you will eventually get in*

# Chapter 18

# STILL ASKING, STILL WAITING, STILL STRUGGLING

The Alzheimer Society of Ireland (ASI) holds an annual Pre-Budget Submission and in 2019 I was asked to be part of the process. Following is the article that I wrote after our work was completed and as you will see, it was also an election year.

Some that attended the submission at Buswells Hotel in Dublin, included myself, as I am part of the working group, and many of my friends who also have dementia. I am delighted to say that it was attended by a large crowd, and I want to thank all of the politicians who turned up and gave us such strong support. Notably, a special word of thanks to our own Michael Moynihan, who is a big supporter of The Alzheimer Society. Indeed, there was great cross-party support and big support from the independents, with the exception of the government. Not as much as one government minister, despite being invited, turned up.

Now just in case you don't know, Buswells Hotel is literally across the road from Leinster House, it's not a 30 second walk. Indeed, we took some of the pictures in front of Leinster House. As the old saying goes, 'they would not cross the road to meet us'. Now I am saying this about the government as if it were a surprise, and sadly, it's not. Last year, we also had a Pre-Budget Submission and not only did the ASI not get any money, but they also didn't even get a mention in the budget, despite promises from certain ministers and giving assurances that we would be looked after. As a member of the working group, it feels to me like they don't care about the 100,000 people currently suffering and the 30 a day who are diagnosed with dementia every day of the week and that is scandalous.

Please, please remember this when they come looking for your vote at the next election. The slogan, 'Still Asking, Still Waiting, Still Struggling' *(ASI, 2019)* speaks for itself, but I will break it down. Our ask is to invest 18.4 million euros in community supports and home care for people with dementia.

**Still Asking** - People with dementia and their carers are still asking the government why no county in Ireland has even a minimum standard of supports and services. The time to provide funding is NOW.

**Still Waiting** - People with dementia and their carers are still waiting for equitable and fair access to the supports and services that they desperately need. The time for action is NOW.

**Still Struggling -** People with dementia and their carers are still struggling on a daily basis, sometimes silently and painfully, due to the lack of services and supports. The time to end this struggle is NOW.

Here is a breakdown of what the money would do.

**7.415 million euros - This to provide a minimum standard of community services in each county.**

The Health Services Executive (HSE) and The Alzheimer Society of Ireland mapped dementia specific community services across Ireland and found acute inequity of services between counties. This investment would triple the number of services and supports available, including an increase of 13 day centres and 118 Alzheimer's cafes.

**1.68 million euros - This will increase the number of dementia advisors available.**

Dementia advisors support people and their families with information, advice and signposting throughout their dementia journey. There are only 9 dementia advisors covering 11 counties, yet the Republic has 26 counties, and demand is increasing fuelled by a growth in awareness attributed to HSE's *Dementia - Understand Together Campaign*.

This investment would mean that families in every county in Ireland would have access to a dementia advisor. Now, if you still are wondering why I am giving out about the government, then this figure alone, 9 dementia advisors for 11 counties should tell you why. With 26 counties republic-wide, more than half of Ireland does not have a dementia advisor and that is not good enough. I am lucky that I have one, and no doubt some of you reading this will know of her and, as I have mentioned before, she is Amy Murphy who works out of Mallow. I can tell you that I would probably not be alive, today, but for the help and support of Amy, that's how important they are.

**6 million euros to develop and expand the number of Intensive Home Care Packages available.**

Intensive Home Care Packages (IHCP) are responsive and flexible, so they meet the often complex care needs of people with dementia. There is an acute need for more IHCPs to enable people with dementia to stay at home. This investment would double the number of packages available.

**2.31 million euros to fund the role of Dementia Key Workers.**

Dementia Key Workers assist people to navigate complex care pathways by providing a coordinated care plan for individuals, as emphasised in the National Dementia Strategy. The investment in this new role would, at a minimum, support people and their families through a difficult health system.

**1 million euros to resource Dementia Inclusive Community Coordinators across Ireland.**

Dementia Inclusive Community Coordinators build the capacity of communities to support people with dementia to remain involved and included for longer. Evidence has shown that the work of the HSE's *Dementia - Understand Together Campaign* is combating the isolation and stigma of dementia. This investment is critical to ensure that this work can be enhanced and sustained.

**These are Facts:**

**1.** There are somewhere between 60,000 to 100,000 people with dementia in Ireland and for every one person with dementia, there are three others directly affected.

**2.** Most people with dementia live in their homes (approx. 63%).

**3.** No county in Ireland provides people with even a minimum standard of community services and supports.

**4.** The number of people with dementia will at least double within the next twenty years and with 30 new people a day being diagnosed, it's a serious problem.

The Alzheimer Society of Ireland is a non-profit organization, it is person-centred, rights-based and grassroots, led with the voice of the person with dementia and their carer at its core.

We had a number of wonderful speakers at our Pre-Budget Submission, and the meeting was addressed by our CEO, carers, members of the board, and by Dr. Helen Rochford-Brennan, who herself is a tremendous advocate and is a voice for us throughout Ireland, Europe and the World. Not only does Dr. Rochford-Brennan have young-onset dementia, but she is also a carer for her husband, and what help does she get from our government? NOTHING!

Helen gave a very powerful and emotional speech, and one of the things she expressed was that she has done a lot for her country and feels her country has let her down, and the one thing that she doesn't have is time. Helen speaks the truth from the heart, and I would advise you to look her up and just see for yourself what a powerful and inspirational woman she truly is. Believe it or not, you can play a big part in helping us by going to your local TD and counsellor and demand that they do something for us. I, for one, will not give up, and the louder we shout, we might eventually be heard.

These were the facts that were presented to the government on that day, and each year it has to be said that very little had been given to dementia services. Each year, we go with different slogans, and in 2019, we chose 'Dementia the forgotten crisis' and it has paid off. As of the time of this writing (March 2021), The Alzheimer Society of Ireland received substantial funding in the last budget as well as a large number of extra dementia advisors who are so badly needed in every county in Ireland. Our country is so rural and there are so many people living alone that it's important that no one is left behind. So, after years of asking and waiting, it has finally paid off, and it could have not happened without the voices of people with dementia, of which I am one, and their carers. If you keep banging on the door, you will eventually get in.

*Kevin Quaid, 2019, The Vale Star*
*(Updated 2021)*

# Chapter 19

## MY BEAUTIFUL DAUGHTER NOREEN'S WEDDING

Today is Friday the 13th of March 2020 and we made it as far as Perth in Australia, to my brother Tom and his wife Julie and their fabulous children, Mick, Sarah, Tom (my godson) and Rob. Tom and Rob were at the airport to pick us up and we came back to a wonderful meal. We were tired but delighted to have made it despite all of the obstacles; my spinal stenosis which I speak about in a later chapter, not to mention the dreadful corona virus.

The news from Ireland last night was frightening; with schools, colleges and large gatherings all closing, people panic shopping and not knowing what the outcome of it all will be. I hope for everyone's sake that the outcome won't be as bad as everyone is expecting, but at this stage, we all fear the worst.

My plan was to stay with Tom and his family for a week, taking in St. Patrick's Day celebrations, allow a day to recover, then fly on to Melbourne to spend some time with Helena's brother, Dave, before going on to Sydney to meet up with the children for the beginning of the wedding festivities. One thing is for certain, you can plan for the future but you cannot plan the results, and how true that was.

Tom and I had been looking forward to St. Patrick's Day for almost twelve months and couldn't wait, but all was cut short. Julie, Tom's wife, is a very dedicated nurse, a person who is sensible and doesn't do panic. She arrived home from work to inform us that all of her ward had spent the day training on personal protective equipment (PPE) and that the hospital was preparing for what was about to come with this virus. She said that she could be one of the front-line staff and, if that was the case, then there was a possibility that I may be in danger of accidently picking up the virus. So, we decided the safest thing to do was to change our flights and go to Melbourne to Helena's brother five days earlier than planned.

We arrived safe and sound at Dave's house and we were all delighted to see one another, but like everywhere, the talk was of the corona virus and the panic buying in the shops. Listening to the advice being given out on the news, we were staying indoors but Dave had to work. Once again, we found that this leg of our trip to Melbourne had to be cut short as there was now a real fear that not only would international borders close, but we were afraid that the interstate borders might also.

At this stage in Australia, all people travelling from overseas had to self-isolate for fourteen days and we were afraid that after coming so far, we could not take the chance on not making it to Sydney. So, after only two more nights in Melbourne, we once again changed our flights and flew to Sydney. What we did notice while going through the airports, was how quiet they were, they almost had an eerie feeling about them; no plane that we were on since we left Ireland was close to being full, a lot of people were wearing face masks and you could see the fear in a lot of people's eyes. It was as if we were all being followed by this terrible assassin who we couldn't see, nor could we feel. What was most frightening of all, is that anyone at the airport could be an unwitting assassin in this terrible virus that has taken over the world.

If you are reading this, and hopefully you are years after it has passed, it is like watching a film about the end of the world and we are waiting for the hero to come to save us at the end. But, as I write, the hero has not been seen and I can tell you that while some people are looking at it as a bad flu season, more people like myself are actually terrified at whatever is coming.

The facts at the moment are that at least 80% of the population will get it, 14% will be very sick with it, 6% will need to be hospitalized and a percentage of them will and are dying. The problem is that the numbers in each country around the world are getting higher every day, and that is of today's date March 21, 2020. Anyway, back to the airport.

When we went to pick up our bags, my son Pat was there to meet us. We hadn't seen one another in over a year and a half, so it was just wonderful to meet him. Pat then drove Helena and me to his beautiful home which is situated about an hour north of Sydney on the Hawksbury River in a very small village with few people, so social isolation was not going to be a problem. It felt like we couldn't be in a safer place in the world, especially with everything that was going on. Although we were feeling safer, we were beginning to wonder if the impossible might have to be done and the wedding cancelled. We initially believed, surely not, but over the next couple of days things changed and people were not going to be able to make the wedding; some because of flight restrictions, some because of quarantine restrictions and some because they were simply afraid for their health. So, the decision was made to postpone the wedding and a new date was fixed for the 11th September 2020, six months away.

At the time of this writing, it looks like after all of the battles over the past number of years, that the dream of walking my daughter down the aisle just might not happen. It's going to be interesting for everyone to see how this chapter will end, especially for Noreen and myself.

Well, this chapter did not have this dad walking his daughter down the aisle. After about a week, we got an email from the Irish Department of Foreign Affairs telling us to get out of Australia as quick as possible as our passage back to Ireland could no longer be guaranteed if we didn't act within a couple of days. To say I was confused, frightened, fearful, and agitated was an understatement. But Helena and the children stepped in and took control of the situation. They contacted our airline and informed them of our circumstances and what the email said, only to be told, 'Sorry, we are no longer flying to Ireland.' Further, they couldn't give us advice on how to get back nor offer us any solution and had no idea when they would fly again. In an attempt to inform my countrymen, I went on local radio stations back in Ireland trying to explain to people what was happening in Australia by giving them the best information available while trying to assure them that their loved ones would be looked after in Australia and would eventually get home.

I suggested that we stay in Australia, but we then worried whether COVID-19 might hit Australia as bad as it was hitting other countries in the world. If it did, then we needed to get out of there because the population of Sydney, alone, is over six million people. So, the decision was made to try and get back to Ireland... but how?

I contacted Michael Moynihan TD, who is in the government in Ireland, and he worked hard for me. I called him a couple of times during the middle of the night in Ireland and his help in getting us on a flight back was invaluable, of which we will both be forever grateful. Although we had to pay an extra 3500 euros for a direct flight, it was worth it to us. So, it was time to say goodbye and get onto a flight in Sydney with a short stop off in Doha and then on to Dublin.

We booked on a Wednesday and were to fly out on the following Tuesday. So, the Sunday before we left was a day that we shed a lot of tears.

I was to walk my daughter Noreen down the aisle and have the daughter and father dance and the song was to be a surprise to Noreen. (The song, if you want to look it up, is by Irish country artist Jimmy Buckley and it's called 'Your Wedding Day'.) So, Noreen and I sat on the couch in my son's house and watched it on the television. We both cried so much because of what the song meant and represented, but there was also that deep down feeling with both of us and we knew it without saying it, 'What if this is it? What if COVID-19 carries me?' At the same time Noreen was thinking, 'Will I ever again get to see my dad?' No one had the answers, and no one knew where all this was going to end.

The Tuesday came and we had to leave, we were leaving our children and grandchildren at the start of a pandemic. Saying goodbye is tough at the best of times, but this time was so different, none of us knew whether or not this would be the last time we would ever see each other again. We checked in and the airport was pretty well organised, only people who were flying were allowed in and all was well until we went to the boarding gate. There were two flights both on the world's largest airplane, the A380, leaving fifteen minutes apart and for about three-quarters of an hour, there were over 1,000 people in a pretty small area. I kept thinking, 'What if someone has got COVID, then we are all infected? Will I be sick on the flight because of it? Will I die shortly after going home?'

We finally arrived back home, and we isolated in our house for the full fourteen days. During isolation, we had all of our groceries delivered and each day passed by and passed by slowly. The only contact that I had with the outside world, was going for a walk about 7 in the morning. That was the time my neighbour was milking his cows and as I would pass his farm, his dogs would bark, he would come out and we would talk for about five minutes keeping at least 40 meters apart. That morning ritual kept me going, and as the days were going by, we were both getting the feeling that we had come through the COVID fire and had escaped. Finally, day fourteen came and no symptoms and no COVID, at last we felt safe. The country was in lockdown, but we didn't mind playing by the rules as we now knew that we were safe.

Day 15 arrived, and you would think that I would be happy, but quite the opposite happened. I think I had a meltdown. The enormity of what had happened hit me like a hammer, and for the next three days, I cried and just couldn't cope. I thought that I would never come out of this depression, but I decided to do what I did after being diagnosed with Lewy Body Dementia and that was to throw myself into my writing and advocacy work.

# Chapter 20

## DEMENTIA AND LONELINESS

I have spoken on a number of occasions about The Alzheimer Society of Ireland (ASI) and the brilliant work they do. I am delighted to tell you that not only is there a working group in Leinster and Munster but there is now a working group in the West of Ireland.

I was listening to a wonderful radio interview on Midwest Radio 96.1fm with one of our brilliant ambassadors, Helen Rochford-Brennan, and a lady named Clodagh Whelan, who works tirelessly with The Alzheimer Society. They were explaining what we in the working groups do around Ireland and that we are looking for people who are affected by any form of dementia to come and get involved with us. Clodagh again spoke about the Freephone number 1800 341 341 that's available to people six days a week. Please call if you feel you can help in any way or if you have any concern about yourself or a loved one that might have dementia. If there is something troubling you at least you will have a person at the other side of the phone who understands, and your conversation is in complete confidence.

As I said, last week, ASI recently published its policy position paper on *Dementia and Loneliness,* and I will share some excerpts from it. The Alzheimer Society of Ireland endorses the following seven recommendations.

## 1. Issue

People living with dementia can experience difficulties when attempting to engage with their previous lifestyle activities yet engaging in meaningful activities can help to combat social isolation and loneliness.

### Recommendation

People living with dementia should be enabled to engage in the meaningful social activities they enjoyed doing before their dementia diagnosis, should they wish to do. Facilitation of this continued engagement in social activities may require support from family, formal caregivers and wider society.

## 2. Issue

For people with dementia (because increasing episodic memory difficulties make reflection on distant events more and more difficult), interactions in-the-moment become more and more important for their social and emotional wellbeing. While people with moderate to severe dementia may forget the substance or content of a conversation, or the interaction itself, the emotional undertone is likely to linger. Interactions that are perceived as negative, off-putting or threatening are likely to decrease the willingness to engage in future.

### Recommendation

Accessible and simple information to help understand dementia should be provided to the general public, service providers, health and social care professionals and relevant volunteer/community groups.

Communication tips and skills relevant to dementia need to be made available to enhance opportunities for effective engagement.

### 3. Issue

Dementia support groups can provide people with dementia, with a supportive forum in which they can discuss the impact of their diagnosis, whilst also providing them with the opportunity to socialise. Evidence varies on whether the format for these support groups or similar interventions should be structured or unstructured. It is likely to depend on the individual. For those who wish to participate in dementia support groups there is likely to be a positive impact on the persons sense of connectedness.

### Recommendation

People living with dementia and their caregivers should be given an opportunity to participate in local dementia support groups. For this, these groups need to exist, and people need to be facilitated to attend.

### 4. Issue

A lack of societal understanding about dementia and the presence of a stigma associated with dementia can impact on the person with dementia's ability to maintain social connections. Furthermore, it can contribute to a person's loss of independence, often making them reliant on family caregivers to help them navigate through social situations.

### Recommendation

It is important that continued attempts are made to address the stigma associated with dementia, at a local and national level.

### 5. Issue

People living with dementia describe how they significantly depend on and rely on being supported by their partner.

### Recommendation

To create a public and professional awareness campaign to raise awareness, not only of the person living with dementia but also their partner or caregiver who may be quietly suffering from loneliness, and to encourage people to make connections with others in their community.

## 6. *Issue*

The impact of loneliness is often rooted in the wider social, economic, political and cultural context. Loneliness and social isolation are absent from a number of government policies, e.g. The National Carers Strategy[13] and the National Dementia Strategy[14]. Equally the Healthy Plan Ireland[15], the national framework for action to improve the health and wellbeing of the people of Ireland does not address loneliness.

### *Recommendations*

To include loneliness as a key priority area in government policies and to raise awareness at a local and national level. Also, to commit to provide opportunities for all individuals to

---

[13] *National Carers' Strategy*. Dept. of Social Protection. July 2019. https://www.gov.ie/en/publication/a1e44e-national-carers-strategy/
[14] *National Dementia Strategy*. Dept. of Health. Updated October 2020. https://www.gov.ie/en/publication/62d6a5-national-dementia-strategy/
[15] *Healthy Ireland Strategic Action Plan 2021-2025*. Healthy Ireland. Updated August 2021. https://www.gov.ie/en/publication/441c8-healthy-ireland-strategic-action-plan-2021-2025/

maintain social networks that foster connections.

## 7. *Issue*

The vast majority of individuals living with dementia are unable to work and the cost of care can be substantial. Families and spouses are often faced with hard decisions, such as whether to admit their loved ones into residential care, seek out private nursing services and/or avail of public supports. Indeed, the provision of care can, in and of itself, be both time-consuming and economically straining. For these reasons, persons living with dementia are more likely to be financially vulnerable and insecure.

### *Recommendation*

The process of securing public support for persons living with dementia should be made as accommodating and accessible as possible for both individuals diagnosed and their caregivers and families. It is also recommended that communities provide opportunities for people living with dementia to engage in community projects and work or services.

As I said earlier, these are the seven recommendations put forward and as you can see everyone can play a big part in what is quickly becoming the new cancer in the world with a person being diagnosed with dementia every 3 seconds worldwide and in Ireland 30 people a day. It's a frightening statistic, isn't it!

*Kevin Quaid, 2019, The Vale Star*
*(Updated 2021)*

## Chapter 21

## AMBASSADOR FOR BLUEBIRD CARE

Here again, is another massive moment in my life since being diagnosed with Lewy Body Dementia.

I was asked by a wonderful lady, Annette Cullen, an employee of Bluebird Care, to become part of their team. I hope you can see from this chapter what the role means to me and what it meant to me at the time to be asked.

> I am delighted to announce that I have been asked to be an ambassador for Bluebird Care and my wife, Helena, as an ambassador for carers.
>
> Bluebird Care (BC) is one of Ireland's leading health and social care providers and was set up in 2007. They pride themselves in providing high quality, safe and effective care in the home and community for persons of all ages with varying degrees of ability. Bluebird Care places the customer at the heart and centre of every interaction, providing care and support with kindness, compassion, consideration and respect. BC provides direct care to customers on behalf of the HSE and other agencies in

This is the same in every house all over Ireland, indeed, all over the world. The person who has dementia is being watched and cared for by their loved one and it's the loved one that is the first one to see the changes even though sometimes the changes can be subtle.

We also spoke this week in Tralee on Tuesday night and in Portlaoise, Thursday night. We're scheduled in Clonmel Wednesday, May 8th and Limerick, Friday, May 10th. Full details of all their talks are on their website and of course, there's a cup of tea or coffee also available on the night.

When a company like this takes the time and effort to give such valuable information to people completely free of charge it makes a person like me who has Lewy Body Dementia feel so good for a number of reasons. It is wonderful to see hundreds of people being educated about the different types of dementia. I'm absolutely thrilled to see them tackling the stigma that still surrounds dementia. There are still so many people in this country that are ashamed or embarrassed by their loved ones who have dementia and, if you are one of them, shame on you. Dementia is a horrible disease, and we need to get the word out there that it's not contagious and it's not our fault that we have it. Remember the person with dementia is not giving you a hard time, they are having a hard time. For those wonderful carers please remember you are doing your best.

I hope you can attend one of these free information evenings and, if Helena and I happen to be there, please come and say hello to us, we would love to meet you.

*Kevin Quaid, 2019, The Vale Star*
*(Updated 2021)*

# Chapter 22

# A SUMMER IN TUSCANY

I have to say that there have been a lot of highlights during the past couple of years, but two stand out in particular. The one that I will share with you is a speech that I gave at a summer school in Tuscany in Italy where we worked with students from all over the world to try and develop apps for mobile phones that would help individuals who have any type of dementia. Our goal was to create apps that might make the life of the carer and the person with dementia a little easier and give them a little more independence. Here's the speech I gave. It's one of many that I have given during my life of advocacy work.

## Presentation to Summer School

## Italy, June 2019

Hi, my name is Kevin Quaid. I was diagnosed with Parkinson's Disease about three years ago and later I was diagnosed with Lewy Body Dementia.

I want to talk to you today about 'the Good, the Bad and the Ugly' side of this disease. I like to remember the saying 'in life it's not the destination that's important but the journey'.

My own journey started around five years ago, although for 20 years now I've had a lot of stress in my life. This led to blood pressure problems which is also a symptom of the Lewy body type of dementia. Although my story is a lot longer, I will start as follows and let you have a glimpse into my world as it is now.

I have mentioned 'the Good, the Bad and the Ugly' and I will begin with the Bad.

### Bad

Bad is eventually finding out after years of searching for what is actually wrong with me. That day came when my wife and I both sat in front of our neurologist, and she told me that the results of my DaTscan[17] were positive for a Lewy body disease. That, with my symptoms, indicated that I most likely had Lewy Body Dementia. I had never heard of Lewy Body Dementia beforehand and like a lot of people I just assumed that a person diagnosed with dementia was having memory problems. How could this be? I had a few memory problems but nothing extreme.

I was also told that it was incurable and progressive... that is Bad.

---

[17] A DaTscan is an imaging technology that uses small amounts of a radioactive drug **to help determine how much dopamine is available in a person's brain**. https://www.parkinson.org/Understanding-Parkinsons/Diagnosis/How-a-Diagnosis-is-Made

### Ugly

Don't be under any illusions... this is one ugly disease and I refer to it as the night-time dementia.

At night when I sleep, I dream about murder, death and all that is violent. The dreams are so real. I had this particular dream where I murdered a person, I don't know who, but I kept going back into the dream week after week and one night I decided to move the body which I had covered in plastic. The smell of the rotting corpse along with the sight of a decaying body stayed with me all the following day. The smell was so bad that even when I was up and awake, I could still get it. My wife, Helena, bought some orange essence oil which I put under my nostrils to try and get rid of it. That's just one of hundreds of terrible nights that I have now... that is Ugly.

### Good

After all of that, it's hard to believe that there can be a good side to this, but for me there is.

I have discovered new talents I never knew I had before I was diagnosed, and one of those is a love of writing. I am lucky that I still have a strong clear voice and a pretty decent memory which helps doctors track my progression with my disease. I kept a daily journal of how my life was going and this in turn lead to my first book called **Lewy Body**

*Dementia, Survival and Me*. To my amazement, I found out that I was one of the first patients in the world with Lewy Body Dementia to write a book from a patient's point of view. I am currently working on my second book on how to live well with Lewy Body Dementia.

Three of the major challenges that face people like me are:

### 1. Hallucinations

These can happen both day and night, but they are not too bad now because I take a tablet for them.

### 2. Suicidal Thoughts

Unfortunately, from time to time, this is a real problem with a person suffering from this disease and indeed, I have tried it myself. Thank God, I didn't succeed. The actor Robin Williams was not diagnosed with Lewy Body Dementia until after his death.

### 3. Fear

This is by far my biggest challenge, and I can be fearful of anything in life depending on my mood.

I am a big man, yet, when I am afraid, I feel like a little lost three year-old boy left alone in a room with a savage dog. That is how powerful, real and gripping my fear can be.

I feel so privileged to be here with each and every one of you.

Thank you.

Kevin Quaid

## Chapter 23

# COLD, WET AND DARK WEATHER IS NOT OUR FRIEND

I think the title says it all for me, this week, as in living with dementia in late Autumn and Winter are very tough to deal with. I find the wet, cold and dark evenings are particularly hard to take and they really take a lot out of me.

The cold seems to get into my bones causing the never-ending pain in my hips to get especially bad at this time of year. Talking to others who have dementia, they seem to suffer from the same thing, and we all agree it can lead to bad moods and frustration. While in this state, I must try hard not take it out on my nearest and dearest wife, who is also my carer, which is sometimes difficult for me to deal with.

To make life a little more bearable for both of us, there are things I try to do, like trying to get out with my friends as often as possible and to surround myself with people who treat me as a normal human being and not the person with dementia. By getting out of the house more, it gives Helena a well-deserved break.

I find that I like to be home before it gets dark, making sure that the fire has been lit and the curtains closed because I am just so terrified of shadows which seems to cause the hallucinations to get worse. The nights not only seem longer, but, in reality, are longer.

To stay healthy during this time, I have attended my local GP and I've found that it is of vital importance to get the flu vaccination. One of the big problems with dementia, and especially Lewy Body Dementia, is if you develop an infection, especially pneumonia. A serious respiratory infection, pneumonia can be particularly nasty and very dangerous. In fact, there is research that indicates that dementia patients may have as much as a 50% higher rate of death due to pneumonia.[18] So my advice to you is to go and see your doctor, sooner rather than later, to discuss the different treatment options that are available to you. If you don't address it early-on you may need to go to hospital, and as you know, these days, the nurses and staff in our hospitals are already under too much pressure.

I can honestly say that once you are in a ward in one of our hospitals, however, the care is excellent but getting past the waiting in Accident and Emergency... well, that's a totally different story. For me, the attention that I have received from my doctors and nurses is second to none and as far as

[18] *Manabe T, Fujikura Y, Mizukami K, et al.* **Pneumonia-associated death in patients with dementia: A systematic review and meta-analysis.** *PLoS One. 2019; 14:e0213825.*

diagnosis is concerned, well Ireland is really up there.

I find the warmth of the sun is definitely great to lesson my aches and pains so getting away for a bit of sunshine during Ireland's winter is really beneficial. It's all about doing what is best for you and your loved one and remember life is short and money isn't everything, so if you can afford it, go and have that sunshine holiday and believe me everyone will benefit from it.

A symptom that may worsen in winter is *sundowning*, also known as late day confusion, and it can play a big role for some people who suffer from dementia.

If your loved one has dementia, their confusion and agitation may get worse in the late afternoon and evening as the sun is lowering in the sky and shadows increase. In comparison, their symptoms may be less pronounced earlier in the day. Some symptoms of sundowning can be seen as pacing up and down, rummaging through belongings, wandering in and out, or seeming to be going somewhere only to find that there is nowhere to go. Shouting and yelling at the smallest of things can also happen and I now find this happens with me on occasion. I might shout at something like the television for no real reason and find myself just confused and agitated. It goes without saying that it can be frustrating and confusing for those who are trying to live with you as well, so it makes sense that it can worsen during these dark, wet, cold and miserable evenings.

Other underlying causes of worsening sundowning can be when a person is over-tired, over-stimulated or they have unmet needs like they are hungry or even thirsty.

In the evening, it might be necessary to reduce background noise and stimulating activities like TV viewing, which can sometimes be upsetting. Other times, believe it or not, the individual may not even recognise their need until they are asked, again a simple question. You might inquire, 'Would you like something to eat, or would you like a cup of tea?' But please remember, if they say, 'No!' then they mean no.

Pain is another factor that may aggravate sundowning. Like everyone, if you are cold and feeling miserable, your pain will always seem that little bit worse, and, again, the person with dementia may not be able to fully recognize or express that they are experiencing pain.

One other thing that may help to lessen the symptoms of sundowning is reducing boredom. I find that when I get bored and I feel like I am not able to do anything, I will turn on the television and watch quiz shows or a comedy of some sort. I also love to do a jigsaw. Other people I have spoken to who have dementia also love to do those puzzle books or Sudoku™.

So, as you can see, the cold, wet and dark days are not our friends, but with a little help and trying to do some simple things, life for the person with dementia and the caregiver can be made a little easier. And remember, please, please ask your friends and family for help, you may find that they are only too happy to help.

On the bright side of things, November is nearly over, Christmas is coming and come early January, the cock-step in the evenings will be in.

*Kevin Quaid, 2019, The Vale Star*
*(Updated 2021)*

# Chapter 24

## HOSPITALS ARE GREAT TO HAVE – BUT BAD TO WANT

I suppose when you have Lewy Body Dementia more hospital trips are inevitable, and indeed, they have happened to me. It's not that I am afraid of hospital, but I have a huge fear around the wait in A & E (Accident & Emergency) which I have had trial of on so many occasions.

On Thursday morning, July 18th, 2019, I awoke to what felt like a crick in my neck, a very severe one. This was not the first time I had felt this in the very same part of my neck (top of my back pretty much straight across from the top of my left shoulder) and was more annoying than painful. So, I got up, had my breakfast, and felt a little sorry for myself because I knew that I was in for another day of pain, while at the same time, hoping it would be gone by tomorrow. How wrong I was.

By the following morning, the pain had worsened, and Helena suggested making an appointment to see my local GP. But would I listen? Of course not! Doctor Quaid here had all the answers. Instead, I decided to take an over-the-counter anti-inflammatory. When this didn't help, I went to the chemist and there I got some rather expensive heat patches. My thinking… well, if they are expensive, then they must be good, even though the pharmacist did tell me to go to my GP.

As it was the weekend, I decided to wait 'til Monday to visit my GP as he may not be on duty 'til then. Since he is always so kind and helpful, I prefer to wait to see him. I applied the heat patches, took my pain relievers and Saturday morning arrived after another terrible night of pain and lack of sleep. I thought… well, if heat doesn't work, then cold should do the trick. So, I went to the freezer and took out a beautiful small fillet of salmon that was shrink wrapped in plastic, covered it in a tea towel and applied it to my neck off and on throughout the day. I knew my home remedies were not working and it was obvious to Helena that my constant pain was getting worse. Every now and then, she would lovingly suggest that I go see my GP to which my reply was, 'I can't be running to the doctor with every little pain and ache'.

By Sunday morning nothing had changed, only the pain which had worsened overnight. When I lay down on my side, the pain would ease a little bit, but if I turned, the pain would radiate out the opposite shoulder. So, by the time we got to Sunday evening, the pain was almost unbearable, and I decided to attend my local out-of-hours GP service called SouthDoc©. There I met a lovely doctor who gave me a morphine injection *(see footnote 1, below)* and said it may only ease the pain but would take me to a happy place and then I should see my own GP the following morning. It didn't kill the pain, but it definitely made it a little more bearable.

On Monday, I couldn't wait to go to see my GP and I was at the surgery literally ten minutes before the door even opened. My doctor examined me and said that he was giving me tablets, one an opioid[19], the other a benzodiazepine[20] and felt they should work within half an hour. Although he thought I would most likely have to go to the hospital, I was adamant that I was not going, so home I went.

At exactly 9.30 am I took the tablets and they sent me back to the happy place but were doing nothing for the pain. I, again, took them at 4.30 pm as prescribed, and at 5.30 pm Helena rang the doctor and told him that there was no

---

[19] **'Opioids should be avoided as they could lead to delirium in *patients* with DLB.'** *(A Healthcare Provider's Guide on Dementia with Lewy Body Disease: Diagnosis, pharmacologic management, non-pharmacologic management, and other considerations, UCSF Memory & Aging Center, Weill Institute for Neurosciences, San Francisco, CA, USA, 2017)*

[20] *'Benzodiazepines can cause extreme reactions in some individuals with DLB.' (Treatment for Lewy Body Dementia, Dementia Services Information and Development Centre, St. James Hospital, Dublin, IE)*

improvement, so he told her to call in for a letter as I simply had no other choice but to go to hospital.

I have to thank our niece, Olive, whose visit was very timely, as in my true stubborn fashion, I had already told Helena that I would wait until the morning to go to the hospital. Of course, Olive convinced me that the smart thing to do was to go right away and was very assertive, so I had no choice but to give in.

As we travelled to hospital, I felt every bump and hollow on the road and I found it a very tough journey. Arriving at the very busy Accident & Emergency department, it was evident that I was in such pain that I was immediately taken into triage and put on what I can only say was a mixture of a chair and a trolley. I was at least thankful that I could recline a little as sitting up straight would have killed me. A nurse took my details and gave me some pain killers (which didn't have any effect), and just over four hours later, a doctor told me that I would have an MRI scan first thing in the morning. Helena decided she would go home, and even though she said she was fine, I knew that she was exhausted not only from such a long day, but a long week. I was thinking if I had taken her advice five days earlier, I would have saved the two of us a lot of pain and worry. Helena is my full-time carer, and to say it's a tough job is an understatement.

Later on, I was transferred to a trolley and finally fell asleep in the early hours of the morning, but before long, I awoke in terrible pain. Eventually I had the MRI scan, but with all the movement as I was being wheeled back to my ward, the pain was becoming unbearable. I explained, once again, amidst my tears, that I had Lewy Body Dementia and was very fearful it was being made worse by this unbearable pain. I felt very alone in all this as I knew if Helena was there, she would stand up for me. I was then given some stronger medication and I honestly don't remember much more until I was awakened by a nurse a few hours later.

She spoke in a very soft and caring voice and even though I was still in a lot of pain, I was delighted to be there and at least the MRI was done. I was excited to see a group of doctors approach my bed with folders in hand. They told me I had 'spinal stenosis' which is a narrowing of my spinal canal which was putting pressure on the nerves causing so much pain. The plan was that I would be looked after by a pain management team who would sort out the pain and I would then be transferred to a different hospital to see a neurosurgeon.

The doctors and nurses were brilliant, but the pain I had was only getting worse. I spent the next few days meeting different members of the pain management team, getting a few hours' sleep, waking up in unreal pain and pretty much going around in circles. On one particular occasion when I was crying once again with pain, a lovely kind nurse asked the pain management team to have another look at my medications as what I was taking was not working. They immediately got to work looking at the medication I was on and trebled some of the doses and added others. She went on to tell me that she had thrown a lot at it, but not the kitchen sink, and she had that if necessary. She was pretty confident that the medication she was putting me on would work for the pain and help me sleep and for a while it did but when it would wear off, I would know it and especially in the middle of the night.

On the Monday, I was seen by a specialist who gave me six injections into my spine and shoulder. The injections were to take effect within a couple of days and, as I write a week later, they may have taken little effect, but it is only little. Later that day, two doctors came to my bed and told me there was no more they could do and that I would be sent home on my medication. Although they told me that I was on the urgent list to see the neurosurgeons in the other hospital, it could take up to two months to get in. Immediately the alarm bells started to go off in my head, here I was on my own with two doctors who were telling me that I could go home on 30 tablets a day and must take them for another two months. It was in this hospital, exactly 18 months earlier, where a consultant told me that too much medication was bad for dementia, especially Lewy Body Dementia, as medication could worsen my LBD symptoms. At that time, I was on nineteen different medications, and he reduced it to six, now I found myself having to take almost double that and a lot more powerful and potent medication.

I told the doctor of my fears, and her reply was quite startling when she said you don't have a choice really because your pain is so severe. 'You either go home in pain or go home without pain.' I then asked her had she ever dealt with a patient who had Lewy Body Dementia, and she admitted that she had not. I then told her about the consultant I had seen eighteen months prior and that my neurologist was based in the same hospital and that I wanted them consulted before any decision to discharge me on extra medications was made. I also thought of my wife, Helena, who as my full-time carer, needed to be informed of any decision that was to be made. At that point, it was too much for me to take and again the fear took over. I was experiencing rational fear of certain medicines interacting with my type of dementia as I previously had trial of their negative impact on my health. The fears of escalating my Lewy Body Dementia always exaggerates every negative situation.

Helena called up every day to see me at around lunch time and all of this had happened before she arrived, so again, I felt this terrible sense of being alone and I pretty much pulled up the bed covers and had a good cry. However, within an hour, the ward sister and another lady came to my bedside and pulled the curtains. I was thinking to myself, 'What now?' But this time it was like God had answered my prayers and sent me my very own guardian angel. The ward sister told me that I was going nowhere until I was happy and introduced me to a lady called Yvonne, who dealt especially with people who had dementia. Yvonne stayed with me and, as it so happened, she had known of me from a lecture that I had given in the University College in Cork.

We spoke for a good hour, and I told her of all my fears around the pain and the overwhelming fear of taking all the medication. While we were talking, Helena arrived, and she had a good chat with Yvonne as well. At last, I felt that someone was listening to me and not only that, but my fears this time were founded, and I was right to be worried about going home on such a high dose of medication for such a long time. I asked Yvonne would she take complete charge of my case and any decisions that were to be made were to be agreed with Helena and myself. I now had a sense that everything was beginning to come together. And to my surprise the following morning, the doctor who had said 'go home in pain or go home without pain' came and sat by my bedside and was so kind. She apologised for what she had said and admitted that she didn't have a great understanding of Lewy Body Dementia and there was now a plan being put in place for me and not to worry about anything. She was very reassuring, and I thanked her for being so nice to me as it always gives me great hope when someone like that will come back to you and say, 'Sorry, I was wrong. I didn't understand about your type of dementia.' My new best friend, Yvonne, came in and told me that she had organised a meeting with all the parties who had dealt with me, including the consultant and my neurological team who I had been looking after me for the past three years.

I would remain in that hospital for a total of ten days and was sent home with additional medications with a plan to wean me off them while keeping in touch with my GP and Yvonne, in hospital, should I need her. My dosage list was now comprised of two medications to treat my blood pressure, one for my stomach, one for RBD (my sleep disorder), one for cognition and hallucinations, and a combination of anti-inflammatory and pain medications, all totalling 27 tablets a day. That's an extra 20 tablets a day over what is my normal intake.

Now can you see and understand why I was so frightened about being left home on such a large number of tablets and how important it was for that hospital to have a specialist person who understands dementia. She also told me if I ever again had to go to hospital, ask to speak to their dementia specialist. At the best of times, hospitals can be a frightening and an intimidating place, but when you have dementia, it's even worse and, for me, the level of fear just elevates to a totally different level.

I want to thank the doctors and nurses and all the staff for the care shown to me and for that I am truly grateful.

*Update:* Now I'm very aware of how it's of vital importance that I take care of my neck. I get injections for pain every six months, and I have to say, thankfully, it is manageable.

# Chapter 25

## A VIEW OF LBD FROM TWO PEOPLE WHO LIVE THOUSANDS OF MILES APART

I have included the following two articles as they both tell their own story.

I recently wrote that writing benefits me greatly, as it helps to keep my brain active while also giving me a focus as do the quizzes on TV especially **The Chase** (on ITV). I find not only does it get your brain working, but a lot of the time your gut instinct will give you the right answer to a question. This helps me to listen to my gut feelings a lot more and I have found that, more often than not, my gut is right, and my head is wrong.

The following are poems written by two completely different people, one in Ireland whose dad has Lewy Body Dementia, and the other is in the USA and he has Lewy Body Dementia. These two people have never met, nor have they ever spoken to each other. I am their common denominator, as it were, as I know them both and we are all linked by this horrible disease called Lewy Body Dementia. I have asked both gentlemen if I can print their poems. Both have agreed and are delighted for me to do so.

The first one is from a wonderful, selfless man in America named Bill Cramer. Bill constantly reaches out to those who suffer from LBD and is constantly offering help and support. If you are in trouble in the dead of night, as I have been, you can reach out to Bill on social media and he is just like a rock, even though he may be having a tough struggle himself with the Lewy bodies in his brain. But, as I said, he is selfless.

Bill put pen to paper and is the author of the following:

### *WHO AM I?*

*I hear the clock it's a ticking*

*As time is passing by*

*I stare into the mirror and ask*

*WHO AM I?*


*I used to know a lot of things*

*Now that seems so long ago*

*Some days I hear and see things*

*And wonder if they are so*

*WHO AM I?*


*I know I am not the me I was before*

*I also know I'll never be that person anymore*

*You see that all changed the moment*

*Dementia came to my door*

*The old me had a good job*

*And lots of very good friends*

*But since dementia came knocking*

*Seems that all came to an end*

*Lewy Body Dementia is what is in my brain*

*It makes me ask*

*WHO AM I?*


*I'll never be the same*

*This disease not only*

*Takes its toll on me*

*It also has affected*

*My entire family*

*Most things I used to do*

*Are now done by my wife*

*It's sad how the plans you make*

*Turn out in real life*

*WHO AM I?  is a question I ask myself
each day*

*I haven't got an answer*

*But I know I'll be ok*

*Someday soon dementia will take away
my brain*

*And at that point I'll never ask WHO AM
I again*

**Written by William Cramer
October 2017**

That is how Bill feels about Lewy Body Dementia as he is living with this disease on a daily basis.

The next poem was written by a wonderful gentleman whose dad is in a care home facility and, like I said last week, the final straw was when his wife passed away and his family, who loved him dearly, had no other option but to put him in a wonderful dementia care home for his safety. His son, Ken, has put pen to paper, and this is how he feels now that his dad has dementia.

I have met Ken and his lovely wife, Claire, and I can tell you that he is heartbroken watching on at what Lewy Body Dementia is doing to his dad. But he is able to see his dad and not just the disease. He is a credit to his wonderful father, and a man who I am glad to call my friend.

### *Dear Dementia*

*D. of Dementia you may feel is for death, destruction & doom, the desolation of a person that dies deep inside daily.*

*However, the D for me is dear Dad do not despair for Dementia does not decide or define whom I see you to be lately.*

*E. is not for each and every episode that eats my heart with envy, envy of those who experience exactly what it's like to have their Dad whole.*

*E for me is an elevated sense of ease, every time you enter a room & encourage me to allow a better version of myself to unfold.*

*M. does not constitute for me a man who may mumble and mutter, who messes food upon his face or who sometimes murders social space.*

*But M for me is the magic you bring to my life, always motivating my memory of our Mom teaching me to make the most of moments, I sometimes see as strife.*

*E. again is not repeating itself the way you sometimes express exactly the same expectation of impending fear.*

*The E for me means, once more you are exactly the example of a Dad I encourage into my life, a Dad I hold so dear.*

*N. can never negate or berate the nature of who you really are, or who you truly would like to be.*

*The N for me neutralises all the nuances and nuisances of those who may never clearly be free, because they fail to see.*

*T. does not represent the tick tock of the talking clock that tries to tear you down one second at a time.*

*The T for me today tells me that this day is the only day, that I must without fear say to you, Dad you truly are uniquely sublime.*

*You are a man that dares to defy that ticking clock and makes peacetime his pastime.*

*I. shall never injure nor impeach the essence of who you are, nor can it inject instances of ignorance and ill will to those that stand afar.*

*Let those who could not accept nor comprehend, implode upon themselves when you finally say, 'Au revoir'.*

*A. Dementia eh! A place in time that will account for all the wonderful lessons that you taught me, all the aces that you never played & all the adventures that you never made.*

*All the amazing things you could have achieved if not for the passing of Mom & if not for how Dementia so rapidly deceived. Deceived both you and I that the letters when accumulated aspire to be so much more than the word itself reveals.*

*No Dementia, you are not my Dad. My Dad is all the things in between each and every syllable that you used to bring us down.*

*My Dad represents the men in the middle of your heart De<u>men</u>tia. The type of amazing man that shall forever be renowned - as my hero.*

**Written by Ken Greaney**
**August 2018**

I hope you can take comfort from what I consider two wonderful poems, one from a patient and one from a son. You can feel both the love and the pain equally in both, as they clearly show how Lewy Body Dementia affects the whole family. It is an insidious, complex disease that creates such a lot of pain; mentally, physically and emotionally.

Ken and Claire have become great friends of mine since this article was first published and have become an integral part of Lewy Body Ireland.

**Kevin Quaid, 2019, The Vale Star**
**(Updated 2021)**

# Chapter 26

## A FELLOW PARKINSONIAN WARRIOR

In May 2018, I had a brief, personal encounter with a condition I knew absolutely nothing about at the time, called 'Lewy Body Dementia' (LBD). I call it an encounter because it turned out there was a remote possibility that I could have this awful illness, which is one of four chronic neurodegenerative and more highly progressive illnesses each generally known as an 'atypical Parkinson's disease'. 'Parkinsonism' is any condition that causes a combination of the movement abnormalities seen in Parkinson's disease, however, some Parkinsonism's can be caused by curable or non-progressive ailments, while others later progress onto their own debilitating course with its own unique set of symptoms and outcomes.

Not everyone who has Parkinsonism has Parkinson's disease, my neurologist explained to me as I underwent two weeks of intensive tests at Dublin's Mater University Hospital in the hope that my medical team could figure out, through their skillful, detailed processes of elimination, what was wrong with me. A few months before this, I had reluctantly come to accept that there was something seriously wrong inside my body and I needed to chat to my doctor. The strange symptoms had started to become obvious to me months before I eventually visited my GP in February 2018. Trembling hands, tripping, painful shooting tremors in different muscles throughout my body, chronic pain in my neck and across my shoulders, an inability to control my body temperature, bowel and bladder issues, and a general overall feeling of stiffness in my muscles. I also found that if I stood up too quickly first thing in the morning, when I got out of bed, that a sudden feeling of dizziness would almost cause me to faint.

Parkinson's disease was eliminated as a possibility, as were mild strokes (TIAs), as was Multiple Sclerosis, motor neuron disease, Lyme disease, and a raft of other autoimmune conditions, eventually reducing the possibilities of what I might have to the four Parkinson's conditions: Lewy Body Dementia (LBD), Progressive Supranuclear Palsy (PSP), Corticobasal Degeneration (CBD), and finally, Multiple System Atrophy (MSA), an 'equally horrible' illness which I was eventually diagnosed with. Unfortunately, all four of these Parkinson's disorders are incurable, and progressively fatal. Three years on from my diagnosis, the words 'progressively fatal' still mystify me, as I don't feel as if I am dying, which is the reason why I refuse to accept my prognosis.

MSA is an extremely rare illness, with approximately only three hundred people in Ireland currently diagnosed. For months after receiving my diagnosis, my life went into a downward spiral of anger, confusion, and hopelessness. I just could not get the notion out of my thoughts that I was slowly dying, and there was nothing anyone could do for me to slow down the progress of this incurable monster. I knew that if I allowed myself to continue down that path of submission and apathy, I inevitably would die, possibly sooner than I thought.

The human brain is an incredible organ. It is undoubtedly, and always will be, the greatest invention – if you could call it an invention – that we are ever likely to encounter. The adult human brain is capable of storing the equivalent of 2.5 million gigabytes digital memory.[21] New research suggests that each of our brains may be able to hold as much information in its memory as is contained on the entire internet.[22] Of course, this is the human brain working at its fittest and healthiest; however, when something goes horribly wrong in our brain, the results can be devastating. In June 2018, this was precisely where I found myself, namely, nursing a brain that was

---

[21] Reber, P., 2010, **What Is the Memory Capacity of the Human Brain?** *Scientific American*

[22] Ghose, T., 2016, **The Human Brain's Memory Could Store the Entire Internet**, *LiveScience.com*

slowly shutting down as my central nervous system began to malfunction.

I gave up my work as a radio presenter in Dublin and moved to Cork to live with my partner, (now my wife) Paula. My neurologist had warned me that chronic stress and anxiety would accelerate the progress of the MSA, so it seemed like an obvious and straightforward decision to quit work and to enjoy whatever quality of life I might be able to hold onto, whatever time I had left before my body fell apart, as this illness progressed.

Chronic illness is a lonely journey. Apathy, anger, depression, resentment, suicidal ideation – all these negative emotions are continually vying for a piece of you as you struggle every day and night to keep your mind and body intact. This is one of the realities I have learned since having to readapt to what in many ways is a new life. Your circle of friends shrinks faster than a bubble bursting – until it dawns on you that you never really had many friends to start with. The phone stops ringing. You spend a lot of time sitting in the back garden, watching television, staring out the window, talking to the dog, wishing for the key to turn in the door to signal that my wife is home from work.

Of course, I also quickly learned that sitting around doing nothing is simply another way of saying 'I'm ready to quit'. Early on in this strangely precarious and unfamiliar world, as I eased myself further

An army of two has a one hundred per cent better chance than an army of one.

Shortly after Kevin and Helena arrived home from Australia, we got into our car early one sunny morning and drove the short journey to Kanturk, in the beautiful green hilly countryside close to where my own ancestors once called home. We had the most wonderful day. The moment I shook Kevin's hand, and we hugged, I knew this was a bond that would last a lifetime.

Two years on and it's as though we have known each other all of our lives. We chat on the phone most days. On Kevin's difficult days, I call to remind him that there is a better day only a matter of hours away; on my bad days, he does the same for me. We enjoy our few pints together. Paula and Helena have been a great source of strength and support to each other, which I am eternally grateful for. When I was handed this shocking diagnosis, Paula's life changed as much as mine, most likely even more so. I know it was the same for Kevin and Helena.

Friendship is so important in the midst of chronic illness. Being able to reach out to someone, knowing they understand exactly what you are going through because they are also walking the same path, is often the difference between living and dying. Too many people in the throes of life-threatening illnesses are all too often left to fend for themselves. Families need to understand that a carer's work is never finished, that the life they once knew where they could come and go freely, retaining their own independence, meeting friends, weekends away, and without having to make plans weeks in advance, is gone forever. Carers also need caring, and love, and support, and most of all respect.

I have no idea what the future holds for me. If I am to believe all I have been told by the medical profession, then my future is looking very bleak and possibly very brief. But I do not subscribe to the notion that any medical expert, anywhere, no matter how eminent and skillful he might claim to be, can tell me what is in my future; that's because my future is still only a figment of my imagination. I do not accept the idea of a prognosis. I prefer to take my chances and cast my net wide in the hope that my adamant refusal to quit and submit will yield something positive that might allow me to go on living a joyful life for many years to come - a life filled with quality and strength and friendship and, most of all, love. This is also the life that I wish for my dear friend and fellow warrior, Kevin Quaid.

*Gareth O' Callaghan*

*People who you meet along the way*

*sometimes becomes life-long friends*

## Chapter 27

# GET ON WITH IT

Many years ago, I had a building company, and this guy came to work for me. He'd been recommended to me, and I was told that he was a brilliant carpenter. Little did I know that day, that it was going to become the beginning of a lifelong friendship, which, sadly, does not have a happy ending.

The following article is very personal to me and, as you will see, it describes just how gifted this man is. I said in the beginning that I wanted this book to help people, not just who have been diagnosed with dementia, but with any type of illness that is progressive and incurable.

> It is with a heavy heart that I find myself writing this piece about a good friend of mine, Jerry Buckley, who's from a small village called Freemount in County Cork. For people in that area and indeed in beautiful places like Duhallow and West Limerick, Jerry needs no introduction. You see, Jerry Buckley is not a writer or a journalist nor indeed a poet, Jerry is a carpenter and a very gifted carpenter; a man who always takes pride in his work.

Like I have said, when I was diagnosed with Lewy Body Dementia, I found that I had a love of writing and Jerry found, after being diagnosed with not one but four different cancers, that while he was in hospital, he had a love of writing poetry. You will see from the poem below just how gifted he is, not only at being a carpenter but also at his poetry writing.

I visited him at his home during a break in the COVID-19 lockdown in November 2020, and we had to take all the usual precautions with social distancing and face masks. Jerry, who I had known at that stage for forty years, walked me through what he has had to go through for the past four years of his life beginning in 2017. Now Jerry, like myself, was a good man to eat and again, like myself, Jerry liked a good pint of Guinness and we often had one or two!!! Now, while I still have the luxury of being able to have my meals and a drink if I want it (simple things that we all take for granted), those pleasures have been taken away from Jerry as a result of throat surgery.

As I have said, when it came to work, Jerry was a gifted carpenter. Indeed, he was a gifted builder and to mark out anything from a foundation to a roof was no problem to him. The man had a brilliant head, and the more complicated the job, the better he liked it. He could come up with a solution to a problem that seemed almost impossible to fix, and when I would ask him, 'How did you think of that?' I always got the same answer, with the same smile, 'Shure you know me Kevy,' and he would walk away.

Jerry and I worked together for years, so every time we'd meet, we would talk about different jobs that we did, some funny incidents and indeed some funny characters that we met along the way. He got such a laugh when he recalled different things that happened, things that I as the boss at the time, wasn't to be told but things that we had a good laugh about. I don't think that Jerry ever had an enemy and I never heard anyone ever say a bad word about him, indeed anyone that we ever worked for always made a point of praising him.

When I met up with Jerry, he showed me this poem and thought it might help others who find themselves going through rough times or who think that they have it tough. As this article was written at Christmas, people were complaining that they couldn't get a turkey big enough, or some other thing. Well, whatever problem they had, couldn't be much bigger than the one Jerry had, and definitely wasn't as big a battle as he was having at the time. In typical Jerry Buckley style, and for a man in his mid-50s, all he cared about was helping others and how he might be able to help them get through the same thing as he was going through. So here is the poem that he said was inspired by his son Darragh.

### Get on With It

*I went into hospital on a Friday night,*

*The doc told me to stay, I got a fair fright,*

*The doc found a growth at the end of my throat,*

*I knew I was in trouble; he was writing a note,*

*They put in a pipe to help me to breathe,*

*They said it would also help me to sleep,*

*But now I lie here with nothing to do,*

*Only think of the good times when after a few,*


*I have a nose I can't breathe with or cough,*

*A mouth I can't eat with or tell you to F-off*

*Sometime next week I may talk again*

*And then I will really be starting to sing,*


*My throat I can't swallow, all part of the plan,*

*It's easier for eating that rotten Complan!*

*I am breathing from there now, bit strange from the start,*

*But it might have something to do with my dodgy old heart,*

*I have it four years now, it's a mighty machine,*

*Four stents work for me now, strange as it seems.*

*With some bowel removed, they gave me a bag,*

*Not much of a chat up line when looking for a shag,*

*But with all of these small problems I'm blissful with cheer,*

*To be having a pint at the end of the year.*

*Piped up to me nose from me belly for feed,*

*From my throat to my lungs to help me to breathe,*

*And with two other lines, all the drugs I can eat.*

*With my nebuliser on, sure I am almost feeling complete!*

*People say I've been through a lot,*

*But with great friends and family, I was never forgot,*

*To the doctors and nurses, I thank you sincere,*

*If it was not for you, I would not be here,*

*My son text me yesterday and said not to quit,*

*So, I just have to learn to GET ON WITH IT.*

**Jerry Buckley**
**November 2020**

I would ask you to read this poem a couple of times and try to put yourself in this wonderful man's shoes, a man who I am so proud to call my friend. The sad thing about the poem is that every word of it is true and the only good thing for Jerry is that he is surrounded by some good friends, a kind and wonderful family and a fantastic son in Darragh. To Darragh and all the Buckley family I hope you all can find peace in knowing that Jerry's wish is to help people by encouraging them to never give up the fight and always have hope.

As I said at the beginning, this was written because Jerry wanted to help people who may be worried about small or big things in life.

Thanks Jerry, for your loyalty, your inspiration and your friendship.

*Your friend, Kevy*

*Update: It is with great sadness that I announce that my friend, Jerry Buckley, passed away in July 2021.*

*'...until we meet again, may God hold you in the palm of His hand.'*

**Traditional Gaelic Blessing**

*There is a saying...*

*It takes a village to raise a child.*


*I have another one...*

*It takes a community to keep a person with dementia going forward.*

## Chapter 28

## INSPIRATIONAL PEOPLE

As you can probably see throughout the book, I have met some amazing people. Although there are simply too many to acknowledge, here are some who have shared their thoughts.

I joined The Alzheimer Society of Ireland (ASI) in October 2016 as Chief Executive and had an awareness of the challenges facing persons living with dementia and their carers, both from my work in the public health sector and as chair of a philanthropic organization, called **Genio**.

Before I joined ASI, I had met persons living with dementia and their carers but it was mainly people who had Alzheimer's. The challenges and nature of Alzheimer's are reasonably well known, but I had not met anybody with a diagnosis of Lewy Body Dementia (LBD), until meeting Kevin and his wife, Helena, when they came to our office to meet our advocacy team. That meeting is still so vivid in my mind today.

It was a great conversation with Kevin who talked about this life, his diagnosis, how he came to terms with the diagnosis, why he wouldn't let it define his life, his eagerness to help build awareness of this particular dementia, and how he wanted to help others with LBD. His account of trying to establish a diagnosis, both in Australia and Ireland, was a trigger for me to ask others the same question; given that after diagnosis, he saw it as a positive to know what he was dealing with. It shone a light for me on an issue that is only now being taken seriously by policymakers and planners in Ireland. With those persons living with dementia and carers playing their part in the national working groups, they have now finalised a model of diagnosis and an assessment of the physical and service implications.

Kevin was only warming up to the issues he faced. He outlined for me, in a very vivid way, the horrific details of hallucinogenic nightmares, having experienced these and the associated loss of sleep over seventeen nights in the immediate past. I came to realise, very quickly, that all I could ever do was listen, but I could never communicate the horror of these nights, and I vowed to myself that we, in ASI, would give Kevin every opportunity in our awareness-raising, lobbying and advocacy. He was very honest about his fears of where LBD could take him and its impact on Helena.

I met Helena separately and got a loving story of life with Kevin, but a heart-breaking account of her role as a carer during Kevin's nights of terror. I learned more about LBD from meeting Kevin and Helena that day than I ever imaged I could when the meeting was set up. Kevin and Helena became treasured friends, and our conversations were as much about current affairs, politics, sport, as they were about dementia, but we knew how we could help each other. Some of these events stand out for me.

Kevin was so energetic and worked very closely with us in getting the message of awareness out in society. One such occasion, an interview with Aoife Finneran in **The Irish Sun** on the 3rd of September 2018, described by Aoife as 'a searingly honest interview'. The headline: 'Bad as Prison, Tormented dad who has same dementia which struck late Robin Williams reveals horrific details of hallucinogenic nightmares' captures the essence of Kevin; a family man, with a great sense of place, telling his story in an honest way, linking it with a global figure.

Kevin is a great team player and his performance at a meeting of the All-Party Group on Dementia, (comprising elected members from both of our Houses of Parliament) was another defining moment for me. Kevin spoke to a hushed gathering of members of the importance of communities being inclusive of people with dementia and how he was engaging with his own community in Kanturk. As a result, Kevin feels safe in his hometown and knows that the community will support him.

Another proud moment for me, was attending the launch of a national report on the appropriate prescribing of psychotropic medication for non - cognitive symptoms in people with dementia. Kevin represented the Working Group of People with Dementia, and in the company of the Minister for Health and clinical leaders, brought the relevance of appropriate prescribing to the attention of attendees in his address.

Kevin has not confined himself to assisting in research, policy making, awareness-raising and fundraising in Ireland. He has been a major contributor to international conferences organised by Alzheimer Europe and is now vice chair of the European Working Group.

When Kevin received his diagnosis, both himself and Helena could have taken life a little easier, but they jointly decided they would make a contribution to dementia care by becoming involved with our work in the ASI. I enjoy watching Kevin; chairing meetings, participating in policy groups, being interviewed by journalists, lobbying for the rights for services and supports, and helping us in fundraising campaigns. I remember fondly our first meeting where I came away thinking he has to be one of our voices of living with dementia. It looks easy for him and that is probably because the great thing about the truth is that you don't have to remember it. COVID-19 has restricted his movements but not his impact.

*Pat Mc Loughlin*
*Chief Executive, The Alzheimer Society of Ireland*

❧

I was diagnosed with the brain disorder of Alzheimer's in 2012 at the age of 62.

It is a great pleasure for me to contribute to this book and particularly important that as a person with Alzheimer's, I can have my voice heard about what it is like to live with the disorder.

So, to tell you a little about me as a person. I am from Sligo in the west coast of Ireland and, for many years, lived in the USA and UK. I am a wife and a mother. I worked in the Corporate and Disability Sector prior to my diagnosis. I was a promoter of Human Rights and served on many Boards. My path with Alzheimer's has been one of denial and sadness, to acceptance and living well, to now advocating for the rights of people with the illness.

My diagnosis took many years of struggling with forgetting words, stopping mid-sentence, wondering what I was about to say, forgetting again, and covering up. I can still see the look on people's faces and feel that burning silence when words failed to come. I had to retire from my job as I felt I had no other choice.

After numerous doctors' visits and many scans, I was finally diagnosed after a five year wait; it was a relief as I thought I was going crazy. My journey home from the hospital was heartbreak, wondering, how I was going to tell my husband, son and eight siblings that in an undisclosed amount of time, I will not remember them or all the memories we banked along the way.

The darkest grief descended upon me for a life I would never have; no plans, no strategies… life would never be as it was, and, believe me, it is not. If you were under the age of 65 in Ireland, then there were no services for you. Eventually, it dawned on me, my rights were violated.

In 2013, a nurse suggested I get involved in research and I did through Trinity College Dublin. This is where my journey into light began, leading me to The Alzheimer Society of Ireland's newly formed Irish Dementia Working Group of which I soon became Chair and, in 2014, became a member of the European Working Group of People with Dementia.

Article 19 of the United Nations (UN) Convention on the Rights of People with Disabilities enshrines the right of people with disabilities to live in the community whilst also promoting personalised service. I want to live in, participate in and to feel that I am part of a Europe that respects these fundamental rights, my personhood, respect and dignity.

This is why I advocate. At times it is not easy, as I see the death and destruction of the brain disorder along the way, but I put my emotions to one side and carry on in order to make a better world for others. I cannot stress enough how important it is, as a person with Alzheimer's, to be involved in decision making; I have the experiential knowledge and I want to be part of the solution.

When I joined the European Working Group of People with Dementia, I became Vice Chair for two years, and then Chair for four years. The working group advises Alzheimer Europe on all its activities and I, as Chair of the group, also sat on the Board of Alzheimer Europe. This gave me the chance to be involved in the development of policies and in research in areas which are of huge importance to my life.

I also participated in several important European projects, not only as research participant, but also in the context of Public Patient Involvement (PPI).

I very much welcome the work that the World Health Organization is doing in advancing the knowledge about brain disorder under the umbrella of dementia. By developing the Global Dementia Observatory, it will allow for an exchange of knowledge and an opportunity to learn from one another. It's an honour for me to contribute to the Knowledge Exchange group.

Alzheimer Europe's strategic plan emphasises the importance of adopting an ethics and rights-based approach to dementia. I had the pleasure to be a member of the expert group addressing disability, which is a topic that is close to my heart, having worked for several years in the field of disability and human rights. And, more recently, to the ethical implications of legal capacity. I have participated in all kinds of research from pharma to academia and much more. Today, I am a Global Alzheimer Ambassador promoting personhood and change in how people with dementia can continue to be active citizens in their communities with the appropriate support.

I have met so many amazing people who have supported me and given me the strength to carry on with my advocacy work, which is empowering. It gives me a sense of purpose and HOPE, and HOPE is all I have as there is no cure for my illness.

With the support of my colleagues in Ireland and Europe, my life has gone full circle from sadness and despair to being the first person in Ireland to appear nervously on national television to say I had Alzheimer's; which I know today gave others hope. Today, I appear in all sorts of media throughout Europe and beyond.

I am honoured to have received awards for my advocacy work on the Rights of People with Dementia.

- 2018, The Spirit of Sligo Award
- 2018, Sligo Business Community, Lifetime Achievement Award
- 2018, National University of Ireland, Honorary Doctor of Laws
- 2019, The Sunday Independent/Gala Inspiration Award, one of Ireland's most inspiring people.

I will carry on advocating; I want my legacy to be that I have done all that I can, for as long as I can, for others.

*Helen Rochford-Brennan, PhD*
*Chair, European Working Group of People with Dementia*

*'Fair play for ringing'* said the lively voice at the other end of the phone.

It was February 2018, and I was making my first call to recruit members for the Southern Branch of the Irish Dementia Working Group.  The moment I spoke to Kevin, who had been referred by his Dementia Advisor, I knew we were going to be collaborators.

To be a member of the Irish Dementia Working Group you must be aware that you are living with dementia and be willing to talk about your experience. It was Kevin's willingness to talk and his fearlessness in sharing the dark details of life with Lewy Body Dementia that made him a perfect advocate.

Kevin came to his first Irish Dementia Working Group meeting and was brimming with humour and honesty. He told me he had gone *'stone mad'* for writing and he shared his plan to write about Lewy Body Dementia. Kevin could see there was a lack of information about the condition but more importantly a lack of hope.

It is now more than three years since that first phone call when I was new to my role supporting the Irish Dementia Working Group and my work with Kevin has been a wonderful learning experience.

I have learned that speaking truth to power takes support. Kevin has spoken to Government Ministers, clinicians and academics. He has been searingly honest and willing to take on tough conversations. But to do that he needs the safety net of his Irish Dementia Working Group colleagues and The Alzheimer Society team. Kevin has clearly explained the support he needs and has created frameworks that benefit other advocates.

I have learned that our high-profile advocates are on somewhat of a rollercoaster. Kevin enjoys speaking publicly, he has spoken at numerous conferences and events, and our team put a lot of work into the preparation. However, I know from working with Kevin that support after the event is just as important. There is often a low after the high of public speaking. Kevin has shared that low with me and I am grateful that I can incorporate that learning into how I support other advocates.

I have also learned about boundaries. In our work together I ask Kevin to share the intimate details of his life. He speaks openly about his dementia, his mental health struggles and his family. What Kevin shares is powerful and personal, and I cannot receive that information without sharing something of myself. We talk about family and pets and holidays and nights out but we both know to keep something back. Navigating this deeply personal but professional relationship with Kevin has taught me that boundaries do not have to be cold or impersonal.

I have learned about the power of humour in advocacy. I imagine many people writing about Kevin will speak about his laugh or his smile or his easy manner and good humour and it is at odds with the darkness of dementia. I believe humour is Kevin's superpower. His positive approach and sense of humour brings out the best in people. His fellow advocates and professional collaborators love working with Kevin and that makes him an extremely effective advocate. I often look back on our meeting notes and marvel what I agreed to as we laughed!

Finally, I have learned that dementia is, as Kevin's wife Helena says, *'a family disease'*. Kevin is a product of his home, his family, his life experience and, most critically, his marriage. On Kevin's diagnosis, Helena became his supporter and his family carer, but she also became an advocate. Together Kevin and Helena are a powerful team, and Helena ensures that the voice of family carers is heard. Lewy body dementia can be a frightening illness and Helena manages to discuss the tough reality and describe the struggle with grace and hope. Kevin Quaid is unique, but I wish he wasn't. People living with dementia having their voice heard and being robust members of the dementia advocacy and research community should be commonplace, but it is not. However, Kevin's strength, humour and relentless campaigning is paving the way for others to have their voice heard. And for that I am very thankful.

*Clodagh Whelan*
*Advocacy Manager, Irish Dementia Working Group*
*The Alzheimer Society of Ireland*

I met Kevin and Helena Quaid for the first time just before Christmas, literally a few days before Christmas on Monday 21st December 2020. The Zoom™ meeting had been arranged by Professor Iracema Leroi who had an idea to start a new group in Ireland to raise awareness of Lewy Body Disorders (LBD). Also at that meeting was Angela Taylor whose father had been diagnosed with LBD twenty years ago – Angela was a principal in founding the Lewy Body Dementia Association in the USA. Iracema's plan was to start an interest group in Ireland and had asked me to consider interviewing Kevin and Helena on my **Near FM 90.3** radio programme to raise awareness of Lewy Body Disease.

A week after Christmas, I watched 'Robin's Wish' a film made by Tylor Norwood about Robin Williams and his struggle with LBD. The tragedy for Robin was that he wasn't diagnosed until his autopsy and committed suicide at the age of just 63.

Maybe it was the fact that this was our first Christmas without my beloved brother Michael who died suddenly from heart disease two months after his 65th birthday, or maybe it was because this was our first Christmas in a pandemic when we couldn't meet friends or family and the only social contact we had was on Zoom™, that these two encounters with Robin and Kevin made such an impact. All I knew was that our next meeting on 8th January 2021, Iracema and I had made the decision to set up a new charity called **Lewy Body Ireland**!

Amazing people were gathered from the UK and Ireland to form this stakeholder task force with a mission to make the island of Ireland one of the centres of excellence for the detection, treatment and management of Lewy Body Disease in the world! And that's the plan – with Kevin and Helena Quaid at the centre!

Since January I've spoken to Kevin almost every day; on the phone, by text, online or by email. I am in awe of his enthusiasm to get **Lewy Body Ireland** off the ground. He has been my guest on radio with Professor Ian McKeith, world expert on Lewy body disorders, and Tylor Norwood who wrote and directed **Robin's Wish**. Helena, Tylor and Kevin all recited poems that day, written specially for this radio programme **Talkin' About Neurodegeneration**. Kevin has a very special way of connecting with people – he is open, funny, honest, raw and emotional – a very special mix.

Kevin has charmed Kunle Adewale, the Nigerian dementia-inclusive GBHI Senior Fellow who donated a portrait of Robin Williams to his widow Susan Schneider Williams, which hangs in the entrance of their home in California. The very essence of Kevin is captured on the front cover of this book, it exudes joy, effervescence, bonhomie and good humour. Helena is there throughout, his constant companion, his safety net and his support ladder.

Although most of this stakeholder group has never met in real life, we are very connected. We meet online and share stories and experiences of living with Lewy. Jacqui Cannon, CEO of **The Lewy Body Society** of the UK shares stories of how she cared for her dad, and her friend and colleague, Christine Maddocks, is a wonderful ambassador for living with LBD. Ken Greaney tells the story of his experience meeting Kevin when he came to visit his father, Dave, at the CareBright Community (the first person that Kevin had met who also had LBD), Joan Hughes tells the story of her mother being brought from pillar to post for even longer. Even though Joan asked several clinicians if her mam had LBD over the course of fifteen years, it was only when they met Professor Iracema Leroi at the Mind and Movement Clinic in St James's Hospital Dublin that they finally received a diagnosis of LBD.

And so, it is now my mission is to raise awareness of this dreadful disease. As this book goes to press, we have just received fantastic news that Dementia Trials Ireland (DTI) led by Professor

Iracema Leroi, Trinity College Dublin, has been granted one million euro to conduct pharmacological and non-pharmacological dementia trials in Ireland. This 5-year study commencing in November 2021 aims to triple the number of clinical trials available for people with dementia in Ireland by 2026.

I hope that after reading this book, you will have learned a little bit more about 'Living with Lewy' which was the working title of this book before Kevin met Tylor who said that Kevin reminded him of Robin, and Helena reminded him of Susan. As compliments go, they don't get much better than that! It has been my honour and my privilege to learn so much from Kevin, Helena, Iracema, Ian, Jacqui, Christine, Ken, Claire, Joan and all the people who live and work with LBD. Angela Taylor started a movement in 2003 beginning with a Facebook™ page, this message has now spread through 'outreach, education and research' to states all around the USA. Our mission is to start the conversation about Lewy Body Disease, beginning with this book – *I am KEVIN! not Lewy*.

The day you came into our lives, Helena and I will forever be grateful.

*Karen Meenan*
*Senior Atlantic Fellow, Global Brain Health Institute*
*(GBHI) Trinity College Dublin*
*Researcher, Producer and Presenter, Near FM 90.3*

# Chapter 29

## RESEARCH AND PERSON PUBLIC INVOLVEMENT

I have had the pleasure of working with so many wonderful people and here are the thoughts of just two, Dr. Andrew Wormald and Dr. Laura O' Philbin, who, not only am I delighted to have worked with them, but also to call them my friends. I am also proud that they have contributed to my book.

෴

I first met Kevin, or rather, I have never physically met Kevin, I virtually met him in November 2019. I was living with a fractured spine, and Kevin was living with Lewy Body Dementia. Whilst, it was clear I had a fracture, and I garnered sympathy by the bucket load; to look and deal with Kevin, nothing in his cheerful manner and his keen intellect would even hint at dementia, and so I guess it does not lead to sympathy and support from those, not in the know.

Kevin and I were brought together by an opportunity to plan a loneliness intervention and gain some small grant funding from the Irish Research Council. I had the semblance of an idea of a plan to intervene in loneliness and The

Alzheimer Society of Ireland wanted somebody to develop a plan, but to gain their support, they insisted I run my plan past somebody from their Dementia Research Advisory Team.

When Dr. Laura O'Philbin of ASI gave me the name of Kevin Quaid, I did a quick Google™ search and out pops this published author and regular newspaper columnist; his face and work was all over Google™. I, on the other hand, was a new academic, 'an early career academic' (as you are known in the Universities), but I am in my 50's, and my wife calls it 'a mid-life crisis academic'. I had just one academic article to my name and a couple of magazine articles. The sight of Kevin's feedback was intimidating, and this caused me dissonance. I could not put together this successful person I saw on Google™ with my experience of people living with dementia, which consisted of people in the late stages of dementia supported by media-fed stereotypes. It was a cold November day when I plucked up the courage to have my first Zoom™ call with Kevin. It may have been the copious amounts of pain killers I was taking, but really, I am confident that it was Kevin's engaging personality, energy and vigour that immediately put me at ease and made me realise we were going to work well together. I knew Laura had chosen well, as we are both of a similar age and similar backgrounds and could relate to one another. The only thing that separated us was that, as I had collected my PhD, Kevin collected his diagnosis. Still, those differences are what had brought us together. When it came down to it, we were two middle-aged men living in the mid-west of Ireland doing what we could to make sense of life and trying to improve the lives of others.

Together, we set out to create a pilot study. We negotiated ideas and threw them backwards and forwards. There were meetings and tic-tacing by email. Eventually, between us, we drew up a plan that we thought would work. By the time we submitted the application, my stereotypes had been totally destroyed. People living with dementia were not these permanently forgetful and confused people. They were just people.

To be honest, after I submitted the grant application to the Irish Research Council, I forgot about the project, since I didn't really expect it to be successful. But, to my delight, yet concern, on March 18th, 2020, I received the news that we had been awarded our small grant. (I mention the date because this award is five days after schools and colleges have been closed due to COVID-19, and I was then back in my home office, and now must sit down and work.)

First, we immediately had to decide if the intervention could go ahead, or should we delay it or change it? Between the three of us (myself, Kevin and Laura), we decided to make this an online intervention that was still going to be small scale. Five to ten people were to be supported by volunteers, and we would train and visit virtually. (The initial plan was to have a volunteer visit a person living with dementia once a week for ten weeks.) Using the principles of person-centred planning, they would agree with the person of one small change that could improve their lives. It was simple, and potentially, it could be amended, and it was scalable. The Alzheimer Society arranged volunteers and participants, and Kevin and I worked on the training. At this point, I must mention two sources that reduced the training workload tremendously. First is Professor Brian Lawlor from Trinity College Dublin, who had previously run a loneliness intervention **Only the Lonely**[23] who allowed us to use his training materials. The second help came from the Befriending Networks, Ltd in the UK, which allowed us to use their training videos.

The training was where Kevin really came into his own. We had divided the training between us, and we were supported by University of Limerick (UL) student, Beverly Hoban. So, whilst I did the routine bits, Kevin held centre stage, charming and giving confidence to the volunteers. For most volunteers, this was their first time dealing with a person living

---

[23] **Only the Lonely: a randomized controlled trial of a volunteer visiting programme for older people experiencing loneliness**. (Lawlor, B.A., Golden, J. et al, November 2014, www.researchgate.net)

with dementia, and Kevin was breaking down barriers and stereotypes. At the end of the training, Kevin's masterstroke was played, offering every volunteer the chance to do a test call using him as the guinea pig. In the follow up, every volunteer said this was extremely beneficial. As far as I am aware, every volunteer took up the opportunity and was far more relaxed and ready to talk to the participants on their first call.

Over the summer, the project ticked away, and we both worked on supporting the volunteers and, eventually, the intervention was over, and data was being returned by the volunteers.

In the autumn, we held two focus groups, one for the volunteers and one for the participants. In both groups, we were well supported by another UL student, Kevin Casey. Talking to people is one of Kevin Quaid's many abilities, but when you are running a focus group, you want to let others do the talking. However, people talked and talked for Kevin, and he naturally knew how to draw the best out of them. Many of us don't talk in class for fear of looking stupid and focus groups can be the same. However, dealing with a person who has the lived experience seemed to set the volunteers at ease. For the participants, they were talking to a fellow traveller who knew what prompts to use and when; he had that inner wisdom that can only be gained through lived experience.

Since the focus groups, we have both been busy working on our own projects and coming together to talk at webinars and give a joint conference presentation. We have not written the paper yet, but we will.

All was winding down, and I was reflecting on the wonderful experience of working with Kevin and wondering what we could do together next. Then, out of the blue, Kevin contacted me, saying, 'I am starting **Lewy Body Ireland**. Do you want to join us? We are having a meeting on Friday.'

Intrigued and wanting to help Kevin, (everybody wants to help Kevin as his enthusiasm and ideas draw you in) I attended on Friday to find Kevin had amassed a top team of academics, people living with Lewy Body, carers and other Lewy Body groups.

I was, again, in awe of this man, and, again, I was learning from him. Along the way, I was also sensing that Kevin was inviting me to further my career and increase my network. Kevin's support continues for me quietly and never announced in advance.

I had been struggling at work, my contracts were coming to an end, and I could not grasp other opportunities; I was down and letting go of the academic dream. Then, out of the blue, I receive an email from the Associate Professor of Politics. The email said she had never heard of me, but after attending a webinar, she was going to follow my career; she even copied in the Vice President for Research, who quickly contacted me and congratulated me. When I looked at the list of speakers at the webinar, there was Kevin Quaid front and centre. The following week my contract was extended. (I will never know if the webinar had any influence on this, but it has certainly had a huge influence on me. I am back up and bouncing with ideas and energy.)

I have always believed that God gives us each a purpose in life, and an old friend of mine, Fr. John Gott, used to tell me 'God has a strange sense of humour in how he works. He will present you opportunities to shine, move forward and grow. These opportunities will not come in a format you want or expect.' I know Kevin was one of my opportunities; he continues to offer support and counsel and will always be my friend.

I wonder if God has a plan for Kevin. Is his life goal to break down the barriers of exclusion for people living with dementia? Kevin could not have found this path without dementia. He would still be in construction, and the lives of many people would have been so much less, mine included. To this day, I have never met Kevin, yet, he has had a great and positive influence on my life in a very short time. One day we will meet in a pub, in Kilmallock or Kanturk, and share a few pints and Kevin will be helping me again.

*Andrew Wormald, PhD*
*Research Fellow, Lecturer, University of Limerick*

ço

Over the past few years, I have had the great pleasure of working closely with Kevin through his membership on the Dementia Research Advisory Team.

When I met Kevin, his passion and interest in research was clear. He was delighted to participate in every research project and use his voice in any way he could to create change. Although Kevin was used to speaking about his experience through his tireless advocacy, participating in research was something new and Kevin lent his voice to countless research studies across Ireland and beyond.

In 2019, I developed the Dementia Research Advisory Team as part of The Alzheimer Society of Ireland's Patient & Public Involvement Initiative (PPI). PPI occurs when members of the public work in with researchers in setting priorities, planning and managing research studies, as well as, in disseminating findings and putting results into practice. The Dementia Research Advisory Team is a group of people living with dementia and carers/supporters who are involved in research in a PPI capacity.

Kevin's enthusiasm for research and commitment to creating change, made him an ideal candidate for the Dementia Research Advisory Team. Kevin is a natural collaborator, so I worked with him to make sure he felt confident in making suggestions and offering advice, and that he viewed himself as a valuable member of any research team.

I distinctly remember when the concept of PPI truly clicked with Kevin. We were preparing for a conference presentation about the importance of PPI in research. He stopped me mid-sentence and said, 'PPI is absolutely class'. A few weeks later, although nervous, Kevin took a leap of faith and joined his first research project as a PPI Contributor. Kevin brought ideas, validation, fun, practical support and enthusiasm, making both the partnership and project a great success.

Over time Kevin has evolved and flourished from somebody enthusiastic about research to an inspiring and influential PPI Contributor. Research is a catalyst for change, but to create change, people living with dementia and their families need to be part of the conversation. When Kevin joins the conversation, everybody sits up and listens.

The concept of PPI can be intimidating for researchers and PPI Contributors alike, but one of the many things that makes Kevin exceptional is his ability to inspire others. He motivates researchers to involve people living with dementia and their families in their work by being a supportive and encouraging colleague rather than a critic. Moreover, he inspires other people living with dementia to recognise their own abilities and what they can bring to the table in research. Kevin is an integral part of the Dementia Research Advisory Team, and indeed the dementia landscape in Ireland and beyond.

To me, Kevin has always been a wonderful source of advice and fun. He is a true pleasure to work with and I am grateful to learn from him and laugh with him. Kevin gives a piece of himself to every speech, meeting, project and research proposal; such is his passion for improving life for all people affected by dementia.

Kevin's voice is powerful, yet humble, and he has used adversity to power real and sustained change, touching countless lives across the world. It's safe to say that we can all take a leaf out of Kevin's book (literally!).

*Laura O'Philbin, PhD*
*Research and Involvement Lead*
*The Alzheimer Society of Ireland*

# A Yearning for Our Old Normal

Diagnosis for Kevin with LBD
Brings a shadow of burden that lingers on me
Too many symptoms, delusions, despair
Swimming in darkness I'm reaching for air

This notorious thief of personality and sleep
Proceeding with stealth diminishing health
A rainbow of dreams blown to smithereens
Confronting challenges unforeseen

Shored up like a stepladder not to stagger or
sway
One day at a time... our new mantra
Days dawning with hope inspire us to cope
And rise to this challenge undaunted
Resilient revival, inner belief
Moving forward one step at a time
Leaning shoulder-to-shoulder, support brings
relief

*A new break of day no more disbelief.*

*A Poem by Helena Quaid, the wife and carer of Kevin*

## Chapter 30

## FROM HELENA'S PERSPECTIVE

My husband, Kevin, was diagnosed with young-onset Lewy Body Dementia (LBD) in 2017 at the age of 53 having been diagnosed two years earlier with Parkinson's Disease.

At the time, there was very little information available in Ireland about LBD, therefore we turned to the great resources of The Lewy Body Society in the UK (*lewybody.org*), the Lewy Body Dementia Association *(lbda.org)* in America and Dementia Australia *(dementia.org.au)* in Australia. The information available on their websites was invaluable to us because, during this period, Kevin was experiencing so many symptoms with varying degrees of severity and we needed to find out as much as possible about this particular disease. Over time, we learned that this type of dementia is very much misunderstood and while memory loss has never been a predominant problem for Kevin, it is only now, four years post-diagnosis, that it is becoming an issue.

After his diagnosis, we quickly learned that this type of dementia, unlike the Alzheimer's type, is not really spoken about very much in Ireland. Thankfully, that is all about to change with the new Irish association which is being developed and named ***Lewy*** ***Body*** ***Ireland***. *([www.lewybodyireland.org](www.lewybodyireland.org))*

To our dismay, we noticed a cultural stigma around this progressive neurodegenerative disease. Because of this, Kevin and I decided to make it our mission to broaden the lens of understanding in relation to Lewy Body Dementia and help others with this diagnosis feel recognised. We believe that by feeling recognised and validated, a person will still feel useful and important in this world.

As Kevin's spousal carer, I became very interested in how studies show that carer burden can negatively impact our overall health and well-being. Indeed, burden is not really the correct term as Kevin is not a burden to me. He is my husband who just happens to have Lewy Body Dementia. In this respect, the word burden is used to denote the responsibility carers carry in their commitment to care and be there for their loved ones. A study entitled, *'DE-STRESS: A Study to Assess the Health and Well-being of Spousal Carers of People with Dementia in Ireland'*[24] was carried out by Trinity College Dublin and supported by The Alzheimer Society of Ireland. Overall, this study showed 'that higher levels of burden in family

---

[24] *Brennan, S., Lawlor, B., Pertl, M., O'Sullivan, M., Begley, E. and O'Connell, C. (2017)* **De-Stress: A Study to Assess the Health & Wellbeing of Spousal Carers of People with Dementia in Ireland, Dublin: The Alzheimer Society of Ireland.**

members providing care to spouses with dementia, were associated with poorer quality of life and were linked to an increased number of chronic health conditions in the carer'.

I could clearly see that taking care of me was a necessity not a luxury. I found myself searching for answers as Kevin's gradual decline was becoming more evident despite my best efforts. It did help, even on the bad days, that Kevin has a great sense of humour. Laughter is a medicine that has helped us through many a dark spell.

On any given day, I could see that life for me revolved around Kevin's declining health and I found myself grappling with that reality. My own life had become small, and I had become isolated, afraid to ask for help and support out of a pervasive fear that people may think I was not coping with Kevin's illness. What I had failed to realise is I needed help for me. I needed to recharge my batteries and dilute the stress that was impacting negatively on my own health and wellbeing.

One day while sitting at my kitchen table going over my daily to-do list feeling quite forlorn and a little sorry for myself, Dennise, my gorgeous niece, who is also my goddaughter, popped in for a chat. As we chatted over a cup of green tea, I told her that my to-do list seemed to be getting longer and longer, I had been procrastinating more and more, and was stuck in a feeling of powerlessness with no motivation to move forward. Dennise loved me enough to be honest and said, that if I didn't take care of me then I wouldn't be around to take care of Kevin. Her words resonated with me and right then and there it was obvious that I needed to face the fact that it was time for me to take responsibility for me, get off my pity pot and get back to being proactive in my own life. Dennise helped me see how I was already on the slippery slope enroute to carer burnout.

As a Complementary Health Therapist, I was acutely aware of how we store stress in our bodies, impacting negatively on our immune system and how lifestyle is of huge importance when it comes to health and wellbeing. So, I knew a holistic approach was necessary to decrease my negative stress and be more attentive to my own needs. It was time to acknowledge that I had allowed my world to become very much smaller while I was adapting to Kevin's changing abilities. In challenging times, I find as little as taking a deep breath, slowing down and counting to ten does the trick. This reminds me to stand back for a second glance and see the situation for what it is. Any situation in life can be overwhelming at times but I truly believe the right approach is key.

Since Kevin's diagnosis, we have both stumbled and struggled along this road which has presented major life changes for each of us. The cognitive fluctuations of LBD are complex, varied and very challenging at times. A myriad of symptoms can raise their ugly head without warning and can rob the day of its plans and create an air of negativity. In an instant and as if watching a movie in slow motion, Kevin's mellow demeanour changes rapidly, his shoulders droop with that all too familiar heavy, invisible weight and doom and gloom descends like an old familiar unwelcome foe that wraps Kevin in desolation and negativity. I watch powerless as I see him losing his spark, while physical pain, illness and mental darkness engulf him and, despite my best efforts to be there for him, I know this is a walk internally he is doing alone. Kevin has a great insight into this insidious disease and while he explains his auditory and visual hallucinations, nightmares or pain to me in great detail, in truth, I am only a spectator. I can empathise and acknowledge his reality as best I can with unconditional love, compassion, patience and understanding, but I cannot truly understand and that is something I have to be mindful of at all times. I bear witness only.

Kevin has the ability to disguise his disease very well, and in this era of virtual platforms, he has the ability to participate and attend meetings and events with little or no difficulty and is coherent and eloquent when speaking of his diagnosis.

Other meeting participants, however, tell me that some days his furrowed brow is the sign of a bad day that is being hidden beneath words, smiles and laughter. In the days, pre-lockdown, when in-person meetings were the normal way of working, Kevin had to work much harder to cover up the relentless tiredness and strain this disease takes on both the body and mind. Many times, I am the only one to see Kevin on a really bad day, days in which he is unable to leave the house. When he is sick and tired, his voice changes to one of weakness where words can be slurred in a hoarse manner. On these occasions he says that he is simply too tired to talk, leading to long silences. Fatigued and weary, he lies in bed until he is once again alert and energetic which is the repeating pattern of LBD fluctuations. He gets very anxious at these times, fearful that his strong voice may not return, while I try to reassure him, as best I can, telling him all will be well as it has been with all such past episodes. Kevin has great bounce-back ability and mostly within a few hours he gets up feeling motivated to live life to the fullest once more.

### REM Sleep Behaviour Disorder

*Nocturnal nightmares of trepidation and dread*

*'Tormenting and torturous,' Kevin said*

*Disturbing, distressing disruption to sleep*

*Vigorous enactment*

*No time to count sheep*

*Recalling in detail all he had to endure*

*Haunting memories on waking uncertain unsure*

*Confused and disordered it's now time for action*

*Time to move on*

*Time for distraction*

Kevin made the decision to retire early from work, Christmas 2017, on the advice of his GP due to the decline of his executive functioning, which is another symptom of LBD affecting his ability to multitask, such as, difficulty with planning and problem-solving. Everything at that time was a struggle for him, made worse by the constant pain. It was evident that the normal daily activities, which added a multi-coloured vibrant dimension to his life in so many ways, were slowly draining away one by one. For Kevin, this life-altering diagnosis of young-onset Lewy Body Dementia was like a thief taking away his independence little by little, especially his ability to drive because of his vivid visual hallucinations and spatial awareness difficulties. He loved driving while listening to the fabulous sound of the great

Joe Dolan. He sang along knowing every word. He loved to dance and was a very entertaining DJ who had a passion for music. Today our home has become one of silence as the noise hurts his brain.

On a good day, Kevin can be very alert, but as the afternoon moves on, he runs out of fuel and then I see him wilt before my eyes. He loses his strength and is left with no option but to rest, but despite his extreme tiredness, sleep eludes him. To most of us, sleep offers refuge and restoration, but alas, a good night's sleep is a rare event for Kevin, and he doesn't get the opportunity to receive its wonderful revival benefits very often. This is due to his REM sleep behaviour disorder (RBD) where Kevin can act out his dreams.

Over time, necessity has taught me the valued tricks of being an excellent negotiator while dealing with Kevin's parasomnia. After a night of threatening and tormenting nightmares feeling totally defenceless, he often tells me he has a fear of living, not a fear of death as unfortunately these sinister nightmares are mostly not erased from his memory on waking and he can be haunted by such memories holding him in bondage even into the following night where he won't close an eye for fear of a return to the same nightmare. After a bad night, he will often say 'if I could wake up dead, I would wake up happy'. He never shares with me the full extent of what happens in these nightmares as he wants to shield me from the details, but he will often talk about their treacherous nature and how cruel, malicious and abusive they can be. While I don't suffer through his actual nightmares, they impinge on my life as I watch on helplessly while Kevin battles through another one of his nocturnal nightmares, not knowing where he is, what he is doing and, most stressful of all, questioning.... 'Who am I?'

I've come to appreciate the dawn like never before as the new dawn brings us hope for a better day, which, of course, never fails to deliver. As Kevin says himself, 'Nothing could be as bad as a bad night in Kevin's world.'

We have been so lucky to have wonderful family, friends and neighbours. Collectively, they have enabled us to distance ourselves as much as possible from this onerous disease. Our GP put us in touch with our local Dementia Advisor, who works with The Alzheimer Society of Ireland, Amy Murphy. She came into our lives when we needed her most and she was an absolute godsend.

Amy directed us onto the right path, and, through her timely intervention, we both became advocates with The Alzheimer Society of Ireland (ASI) and, from there, our lives changed, due to this positive distraction, giving us a sense of inclusion and involvement. I joined the Dementia Carers Campaign Network (DCCN) and met Laura

Reid who was the Advocacy, Engagement and Participation Officer and, as such, she had a particular responsibility for the management and development of the DCCN. Laura helped me so much with her friendly, kind and caring approach. Thank you, Laura for all your help.

For a while after diagnosis, LBD coloured our experience of daily life in a negative way but, as time went on and with the outside distraction of our advocacy work through The Alzheimer Society, acceptance brought gratitude and once again the colours of life returned, one by one, as belief brought hope, and hope shone a light on a pathway to a brighter future. Slowly life, once again, started to ebb and flow but at a different speed. A new normal with little glints of sunshine that brought joyful anticipation and a move away from the heavy cloud of Kevin's anticipatory grief which only allowed him to focus on the incurable and progressive nature of his diagnosis. This anticipatory grief did nothing but feed his imagination in a negative way, which for him, was depressing, distressing and demoralizing. As his wife, I can now admit openly that I also certainly suffered from this contagion but, at the time, my denial obscured my view of this reality.

Living with Lewy Body Dementia, it is clear to see, that the only certainty is uncertainty. The great lyricist, songwriter and singer, Donovan, says it really feel the benefits. In addition, I love gardening and our garden is my escape to a level of serenity I couldn't find anywhere else. I find listening to the birds or simply looking at nature's repeating patterns uplifting and peaceful. When I say I escape to the garden, I mean for me, this is as a brief relief from reality. I'm not running away from reality, such as living in denial, but it's more of an acknowledgement of our reality and the need to get into the real rhythm of life through nature. I can easily get bogged down in the sticky bog land of LBD and, as we have no hired outside help, I am so lucky to have gardening as a lovely distraction.

I enjoy being outdoors in such a tranquil space listening to the birds and watching the visiting neighbour's cat when she is on the prowl, totally unaware of my presence. Pottering in the shed on a cold winter's day with the rain beating like a drum on the corrugated roof echoing each ripple in its valleys, never the same, but with a rhythm all its own. My ritual sets me up for a good day and I find it helpful to do the most important things first, always doing my best to live in the present moment. As my dad always said, *'Yesterday is history, tomorrow is a mystery, so stop rushing today.'* When I do that, I can cope with anything.

### Rhythm, Ritual & Routine

*The rhythm of nature*

*Echo sounds of sincerity*

*In silence, collaborating with what is unseen*

*Its collective heart is steadily beating*

*Living by rhythm, ritual and routine*

*Ritual differs as much as humanity*

*Births, deaths and marriages*

*With hope in between*

*Carved out traditions of custom and culture*

*Living with rhythm, ritual and routine*


*A daily routine of work, rest and sleep*

*Help life's jigsaw fit snugly*

*And work like a dream*

*Alive for today, so don't get bogged down*

*Living is rhythm, ritual and routine*

# Chapter 31

## GOLDEN NUGGET MEMORIES

Sometimes when I write, I can find it hard to start off a chapter or even a sentence. Is that what they call writers block? But then, thankfully, as I sit at my computer, it's like a switch is turned on and words just seem to flow with ease. At times I can even find that I'm getting ahead of myself, by that I mean, I will have so much to say that when I look back on what I have written it can be full of half sentences and full of beginnings to untold stories. This has often got me thinking, is it my dementia or is it the normal process of aging? The wonderful thing about it is when I look back on what I have written, I am reminded of what I was going to say and then I am able to finish it.

Being able to recall my storylines is of wonderful value to a person like me who has dementia even though, as I have often said, the fact that I have Lewy Body Dementia doesn't cause me too many memory problems. Nowadays, I am becoming more aware of it especially with my short-term memory or, as I like to call it, my immediate memory.

I am a fan of horse racing but not a very big gambler. I get excited at a race when I have a 5 euro each-way bet, and last of the big spenders I hear you say. I could see a horse on television I think has a chance of winning, and if I decide to bet on it, immediately I can't remember the name of the horse, the number of the horse, the jockey or the jockey's colours. To combat this, I always write it down as soon as I have it done, or if there is someone with me, I will tell them what I have backed and I ask them to remind me.

It's easy for me now, but at the start, I was a little embarrassed to ask and I hated saying, 'I just backed number 9, will you remind me?' I also felt the need to apologise and to say that my memory wasn't great because I had dementia, and looking back on it now, it seems as if I was apologising to my friends for having dementia. I don't do that anymore because my friends know, and it is now just a part of life. Indeed, if I don't tell my friends what I've backed, they will ask me anyway… no fuss. It's just one of the many little coping mechanisms that I have developed on my journey with Lewy Body Dementia.

I started off this chapter with the words 'gold, nuggets and memories' because I look at the brain of each and every person in the same way as you would look at a gold mine. In a gold mine are people at work finding little pieces of gold, then bigger pieces until they hit the rich vein, and this is where the big gold nuggets are found. This is what it's all about, finding the rich vein and making it pay and why do people do that? Well, the answer is to have a great life with lots of choices that success and fulfilment can bring.

Then there are gold mines that provide very little, or indeed, they are not properly explored, and people give up. But maybe if they kept going that little bit further, they would have found that rich vein. For those who give up, the mine is abandoned, and the mine shaft not used, and it is just left there and for most people forgotten about. I think that it is the same for us, humans; some people use their brain wisely and can reach their full potential in life, while others just plod along and do enough to get by and in both cases that is OK.

So, imagine what it is like for a person who has dementia, and we will go with someone who has had a great life and has reached or came close to reaching their full potential. One day they notice that something is wrong, the mind is not working as good as it once was, they go to their doctor, and they are told they have dementia. It's like the company saying that the mine is going to close. But that is something that I have refused to do, I have refused to let my brain close down. I have days and weeks when things are going bad and I am just not able to do anything, there are days when I just don't want to and then there are the days that I need to give myself a little push, it's like saying go back to the mine and find some more gold nuggets.

People who are in the middle to late stages of dementia are like the mines that have closed down, and many of the people who knew them don't keep in touch anymore except for close family and friends. But when the person with dementia talks, they might talk in riddles, or they might start talking about things that happened years ago and talk like it was only yesterday or that it is happening right now. It is so important to listen, and I mean really listen to their stories, because they will tell you things about the past in such great detail that you will probably hear things that you never knew happened or existed. For me, those memories are the real gold nuggets, these are the nuggets that were left behind when the mine closed but they are still there, and they are pure gold. Remember when your loved one is not able to talk anymore or when they are gone, they are gone for good, so it's then that you'll treasure those golden moments and those brilliant conversations.

I think back to a dear friend of mine in Australia, Monica Stewart, who sadly passed away from Alzheimer's Disease a number of years ago. I used to visit her in Brisbane, and she might ask me a couple of times in an hour the same question, 'Kevin where are you living now?' I would answer,

'Sydney'. But in between those questions were Monica's golden nuggets when she could recall visiting my family in Ireland and spoke lovingly about the holiday of a lifetime she had with us. She spoke about the days when we all toured the 'Ring of Kerry', and she could name the places where we stopped along the road. She could remember what type of sandwiches we had and was well able to remember some funny stories about how my dad was so well able to drive on such narrow and dangerous looking roads on side of the rolling green hills. We were all packed into the van, and those were the days before everything became so strict with rules and regulations such as the wearing of safety belts. Her stories were pure gold and ones that I hopefully will never forget. She was a wonderful lady who raised a large and beautiful family, a family that I am so proud to say are still very good friends with us today.

One of my best friends was my Uncle Dave who lived in Chicago (I also spent some time living there). He passed away in the last couple of years, also from Alzheimer's, and I have again such wonderful memories of being with him whether it was on the golf course in Chicago or just the two of us alone. He was a man that I could talk to about anything and always offered such brilliant advice. The time I spent with him was just pure gold and that is why I say, if you have a loved one with dementia spend the time with them because when it's over, it's over.

I have another uncle, Billy Norris, who passed in March 2020 and to whom this book is dedicated. Anytime I talked with him, the first thing that he always said was, 'How's my favourite nephew?' Even though I am 56 now, when I spoke to him, I sometimes felt like a small little boy again and loved to be told that I am his favourite.

Billy was a truck driver who spent years in the Navy as a young man and travelled the world. When Billy would call, we would all gather round and listen intently to his stories, as he was a natural storyteller, and he always had an amusing slant to every story and always fun. It's a time when our house rang out with laughter and, to this day when having a conversation with his wife, my Aunt Joan, we always end up laughing recalling those times.

For a person like me who lives with dementia, times like these mean more to me now than they ever did. To me, they are pure gold.

# EPILOGUE

This man, with his head bowed as he sat in his chair with a cup of coffee next to him in the CareBright community in Bruff, County Limerick, slowly lifted his head, smiled, and said, 'Kevin Quaid, I thought that I would never see you again.' He then put his arms around me and gave me a hug.

That man's name is Dave Greaney, and I have mentioned his son, Ken, and Ken's wife, Claire, earlier in the book. Dave is now 69 years of age and has lived with Lewy Body Dementia for over eleven years. Over that span of years, both Ken and Claire tried in vain to get his dad the proper treatment. Recently, they were successful, and it has drastically changed him, he looks and feels better.

One thing that Dave has done is put to bed the myth that all dementias have memory problems. You see, I didn't know Dave growing up; didn't play sports with him, didn't have a pint with him. The first time we met was when he moved into CareBright, and he was the first person I met who had the same diagnosis as me. He has the same terrible nights; awful hallucinations and he is very aware of them.

The day we first met, he showed me around his care community, displaying his beautiful room and personal photos, of which he could name everyone in them. But I could see, Dave was struggling with different aspects of his daily life, and since it was only a few months into my own diagnosis, I found it particularly hard to take as it felt like a look into my future. It took me a while to get over those feelings, but when I did, I visited him on two more occasions, and we had coffee and a couple of good chats.

When COVID-19 struck, it would be over two years' time before I would see Dave again and, the moment he saw me, he knew who I was. The next time his daughter-in-law Claire visited him, he told her that I had come to call, and he asked whether she knew that I was writing this book, and he was curious as to whether he might get a mention in it. Even though he might struggle with everyday tasks, it proves to me that his brain, like mine, is still in good shape, although we both have Lewy Body Dementia.

Dave is so fortunate to have such wonderful support in Ken and Claire, both of whom are co-founders of Lewy Body Ireland. And, yes, **Dave Greaney**, you are in this book, as you are an inspiration to so many people, especially me. From the first day I met you, I made a promise to myself that I would fight as long and as hard as I could to keep this disease at bay, and I owe that to you, Dave.

I am coming to the end of my book, and it's been a wonderful and, sometimes, tough journey to get here. I am so proud of my wife, Helena, who is currently Chair of the Dementia Carers Campaign Network, (DCCN) a member of the Dementia Research Advisory Team, as well as my carer and my supporter in my roles as Vice Chair of the European Working Group of People with Dementia, member of the Irish Dementia Working Group, Co-founder of Lewy Body Ireland, and a participant in numerous research projects. She helps me every week with the articles that I write for newspapers and magazines and is always there to support me when on radio or TV.

So many good things have happened in my life since I was diagnosed with this horrible disease, one I wish I never had. I do know, however, that it's not my fault, I didn't cause it, and I will never give up the fight against it nor my advocacy work.

My one wish for you, the reader, is no matter whether you have dementia, are a caregiver, or are someone affected in any way by any disease that you don't give up, as there is help out there. You may have to turn some stones, but reach out, ask questions, and let people into your life who can and will help. My final message to you is that you take the time (if you haven't already) to read pieces about individuals who have made the choice to embrace life. Think… *'If they can do it, then so can I.'* Start with small changes, even if it's just a phone call or an email to someone. And I always leave the door open for you to contact me (*kevinquaid9@gmail.com*).

So, now I will leave you with a prayer that I live by.

*God grant me the **SERENITY** to accept the things I cannot change,*

***COURAGE** to change the things I can*

*And the **WISDOM** to know the difference*

# ACKNOWLEDGEMENTS

There is a saying that no man is an island and even though there are times when my disease really takes hold of me, times I can truly feel alone even when surrounded by friends and loved ones.

But I know that I am not alone, and not only this book, but my life and my very existence, would not be possible without the love of my entire family; my parents, brothers, sister, and my wider family (especially my cousins). There are actually too many to mention, and I could write a book about the support that I have gotten from so many people. I want to especially thank some who helped me put this, my second book, together. They are written in no specific order but, for me, they are due a special mention.

I will refer to, first, the most important people in my life. My wife, Helena, who stares down at the cold face of this disease, living with me and caring for me, each and every day. I simply don't know how she does it. As I have often said, 'it's a lot easier to have Lewy Body Dementia than to live with someone who has it'. Thank you to my children Noreen, Pat and Kevin and my stepchildren Declan, Shane and Michelle for their love and support as well as their outstanding partners. Both Helena and I have been blessed with the most wonderful and beautiful grandchildren, in Hollie, Charlie, Liam, Victoria, Jamie, Josh, and the newest little one, baby Piper.

I want to say a special thank you to the following:

### Helen Bundy Medsger

Not only did Helen edit this book, and did a brilliant job, but went over and above what was asked of her. We had many a Zoom™ call and my hope is that Helen is another person who has become, for me, a lifelong friend. After caring for two generations of her family who have passed from LBD, she understands the many challenges, and her empathy, wisdom and kindness to me is simply amazing.

### Professor Iracema Leroi

I will never forget the day that she made the call to me about starting **Lewy Body Ireland**. It was a call that, until that day, I was only dreaming about. We have a lifetime of work and friendship ahead of us, and I want to thank her for the beautiful Foreword to this book.

### Karen Meenan

I quite simply call this lady, 'my angel'. I am blown away by her offering, '24 hours a day, 7 days a week, please call me.' Her encouragement has quite simply been, inspirational, and the work that she continues to do for people with dementia will never fully be known. I am proud and honored to call her my friend.

### Lorraine Quaid Myers

Lorraine is a cousin of mine, but that just doesn't even begin to describe what she means to me.

First of all, she is a graphic designer, and it is Lorraine, who designed the cover for this book. I kept sending her email after email for the smallest of changes, and nothing was a problem to her. Lorraine is also the daughter of Theresa Quaid Myers, my first cousin, who my first book, *Lewy Body Dementia, Survival and Me*, would never have been written but for her constant encouragement and giving me a push when I needed it. Lorraine is definitely her Mam's daughter, and I can only say that we are so proud and thankful to her and proud to call her our friend.

### Kunle Adewale

Kunle is the wonderful artist who, not only did the painting of me for the cover of the book, but also the painting on the back of the late Robin Williams, which he presented to Robin's wife,

Susan Schneider Williams. In addition to holding a degree in Fine and Applied Arts, he has expanded his education into the field of arts in medicine, and more recently, how the arts might reduce the impact of dementia. To put it quite simply, the man is incredibly gifted and generous at his craft, as well as being a global humanitarian, and truly a lovely gentleman. *(https://kunleadewale.com)*

### The Alzheimer Society of Ireland

Quite simply a wonderful organization and, as I have said on several occasions, one that has saved my life and, my sanity. There are too many people there to speak of, but I must mention a few.

### Pat Mc Loughlin

Pat is the CEO of The Alzheimer Society of Ireland, and I can still remember the first day that I met him. It's fair to say that we became friends immediately, and the extent of the work that he does for people with dementia will never be known, but his legacy will never be forgotten. Pat is a true gentleman and inspiration; not just to me, but to so many.

### Clodagh Whelan

Clodagh is what we like to call in the Irish Dementia Working Group, 'the Mammy'. Although she is years younger than any one of us, she looks after us in everything we do when it comes to advocacy work. If you want a hand with a speech, if you need someone to talk up for you, she will ask you if you would like to be involved in certain projects and has the ability to put you into a project which you will love. Clodagh's understanding and empathy for people with dementia and their carers is second to none and she has often called me on a Saturday or Sunday to see how I am feeling if she knows that I am not well, and she does the same for every one of us in the working group. If I am ever unsure of something to do or say, as far as my advocacy work is concerned, I will ask Clodagh. Like so many more, we have become good friends and she is quite simply a wonderful lady.

### Dr. Laura O' Philbin

I want to thank Laura for the beautiful article she has written for this book. I got to know her when I started getting involved in research and we have done so much work together since then. Laura is such a beautiful person and so full of life; no matter what project we have been involved in; we have fun doing it. Laura is more than a colleague, and I hope that she has become another lifelong friend. I am so lucky that she came into my life.

### Dr. Helen Rochford-Brennan

It has been one of the highlights of my life to get to meet and know Helen and her husband Sean. Helen wrote a beautiful piece for this book, and it is only a brief glimpse into the unbelievable work that she has done for the best part of a decade. Not only was she diagnosed with Alzheimer's, but she also cared for her husband, Sean, who had his own battle with illness. Sadly, since I started writing this book, Sean passed away. I was lucky enough to meet Sean on several occasions and we often shared a pint or two. The word legend is often just thrown about, well in Helen's case that is exactly what she is. Also, the word gentleman is scattered about. Well, when I say that Sean was a gentleman, he truly was. He was the kind of a man that some people could only ever dream about being, and even though he is gone, Helen continues with advocacy work and works with me in Europe. I am so lucky to call her my very good friend.

### Dr. Andrew Wormald

I met Andrew after Laura O' Philbin introduced us to do some research together. The funny thing is, I didn't know what I would bring to the table in his research, and he was just as nervous of meeting me, but within minutes of meeting one another, we both felt at ease. As I have mentioned before, Lewy Body Dementia gives you very few good WOW moments, however, when Andrew told me that he was making me co-lead in the paper that was another amazing moment in my life, (certainly one that would never have happened if I didn't have Lewy bodies). I want to thank Andrew for the beautiful piece that he has written for the book and look forward to doing more work with him. I am proud to also call him my friend.

### Amy Murphy

I have to mention this wonderful lady, who is my Dementia Advisor. She was the first person that I met after my diagnosis and made both Helena and myself feel like that my life was not over and that I had so much living left to do. Amy is a big part of the success of the Kanturk Dementia Café and, like so many more that I have written about, the amount of work that she has done for people with dementia will never be known. I am delighted that Amy is my Dementia Advisor, but even more delighted, that she is my friend.

### Irish Dementia Working Group

This wonderful group of people have become my second family and who I have come to know and love. Their kindness and understanding are what have sustained me since I was diagnosed.

### Gareth and Paula O' Callaghan

I met this wonderful couple as a result of Gareth reading my first book, and we have become what I can only describe as lifelong friends. Gareth has his own battle with MSA (Multiple System Atrophy), and while we often talk and share our experiences, we also share a lot of laughter and fun, and they are a beautiful couple who are always there for Helena and me.

His latest book, **What Matters Now**, is a must read for everyone.

### Ken and Claire Greaney

Two wonderful friends, who we got to know because Ken's Dad also has Lewy Body Dementia. Whenever I am feeling down, I will get a call from Ken, and he always knows the right thing to say.

### Professor Ian Mc Keith

I want to thank him for his kind words and his constant work in the fields of education, research, and program development to help those affected by Lewy Body Dementia throughout the UK and the world.

### Vicky Phelan

I want to thank Vicky for her constant encouragement. Her battle with cervical cancer and her refusal to be silenced, which she details in her memoir, has been an inspiration to many around the world. Her memoir, entitled, **Overcoming,** is a powerful book and a must read for everyone. I am proud to call her my friend.

### Annette Cullen

I got to know Annette while I was an ambassador for Bluebird Care and we have become lifelong friends, hopefully. Her constant support, encouragement and good humour has kept me going through some very dark days, and she has given her time so freely to help us set up **Lewy Body Ireland**.

### Tylor Norwood

Tylor is a film maker that I have had the opportunity to meet with on two occasions. As Tylor was the director of the film, **Robin's Wish**, the story of Robin Williams, his wife Susan, and their harrowing journey with undiagnosed Lewy Body Dementia, he, Professor Ian Mc Keith, Helena, and myself were guests on a radio programme on the topic of LBD.

For the radio show, we were each asked to pick our favourite song and poem, (you have already seen Helena's and my poems in this book) so I think it is fitting to end the book with Tylor's poem.

### The Cowering Bush

*By Tylor Norwood*

*There is a bald hill out in the wilds*
*A place separate from the green fields*
*thick with life bending as one*
*Revealing the invisible currents above*
*But in this place, this dry place, the world is feeble*
*and barren*
*Except for one green, worn, whipped soul*
*One cowering bush*
*One who stands like the last leaf on a tree near*
*falling, yet holding this place*
*The wind making it twist and furl*
*At every invisible lick - it looks near to be plucked*
*But with hope - cowering and holding its place*
*Here as a hero, king, and master of all the pale*
*ground*
*And all for the hope of a seed*
*Some dream of fluff on the horizon*
*Of a sea of life coming to join*
*To, for once, be lost in a powerful dance of life, on*
*life, on life*
*The pulsing that defines forests, plains and thriving*
*places*
*To bend under wind but finding the support of a*
*neighbour,*
*and that neighbour's neighbour*
*Even as its own roots are exposed by the*
*weightless force*

*The one that pulls and whips it,*
*tugs at it*
*Pulls away the grains and clods of dirt that form a*
*hold under its roots*
*Licked by every whooshing wave*
*Washing this once lush bush of will*
*Making a release more and more painless as it is*
*unrooted*
*Its hopeful tendrils push deeper into the soil in*
*dumb opposition*
*- Until –*
*A new fantasy appears to it*
*One of letting go, of tumbling, of rolling*
*Tossing on an invisible tide*
*Joining this neighbour*
*toward that place*
*A husk caught by a branch*
*Pulled to the floor of a lush place*
*Where safe in a world of roiling and rolling leaves*
*This bush can feed another's dream*
*Be brought to the dirt to be part of this teeming*
*place*
*This new fantasy is a sorrowful creeping vine inside*
*the bush*
*Winding through the branches, boughs and*
*bending its roots skyward*
*Wearing it to loose itself from this lifeless hill*
*Falling up to the will of the wind*
*Falling into the arms of a sea of dreams*
*Dying into another's life*

*The cowering bush is here*
*The feeling thing now*
*Alone*
*And dreaming of touch*

Printed in Great Britain
by Amazon